LEISURE

The Nation's Favourite . . .

The Nation's Favourite ...

MATHEW CLAYTON

Quercus

032

First published in Great Britain in 2010 by

Quercus

21 Bloomsbury Square

London

WC1A 2NS

2

A CIP catalogue record for this book is available
from the British Library

ISBN 978 1 84916 994 3

Text designed and typeset by Ellipsis Books Limited, Glasgow

Printed and bound in Great Britain by Clays Ltd. St Ives plc

For Gemma, Laurie and Stella

Introduction

This book attempts to answer a simple question. What are the nation's favourite things? Using surveys, polls, market research and bestseller lists, it looks at everything from computer games to crisps, diets to dogs' names, poems to playground games.

The picture of Britain that this reveals is sometimes familiar, often surprising and always fascinating. As a nation we currently drink more Buckfast Tonic Wine than Harvey's Bristol Cream, as office workers we enjoy our first snack of the day at 10.37 a.m., and our preferred biscuit to dunk in our tea is the chocolate digestive (on average they last eight seconds before disintegrating – HobNobs last only four). We like to moan about the weather, eat chicken tikka masala, and have a very high opinion of Take That – believing that Gary Barlow is a better songwriter than Lennon and McCartney, and that our children are more likely to go to sleep if we sing them the Take That song 'Patience' rather than a traditional lullaby. And while we are now more likely to read our newspaper online than on paper, our nation is still baffled by some aspects of the twenty-first century. The most asked question last year on one Internet search engine was 'What is Twitter?' – only slightly ahead of 'Is Lady Gaga a man?'

Mathew Clayton
Ditchling Common,
2010

The Nation's Favourite . . .

. . . Accents

1 Sean Connery
2 Trevor McDonald
3 Terry Wogan
4 Hugh Grant
5 Moira Stuart

Source: BBC 2005

The Queen and Billy Connolly featured in both the top 10 favourite and least favourite lists.

The least popular accent was that of Irish politician Ian Paisley, while the least popular regional British accents are those from Birmingham, Liverpool and Glasgow.

Sean Connery has also been voted as having the worst ever film accent for his Oscar-winning role as Irish cop Jim Malone in *The Untouchables* (beating Dick Van Dyke in *Mary Poppins*).

. . . Albums of 2009

1 Susan Boyle – *I Dreamed A Dream*
2 Lady Gaga – *The Fame*
3 Michael Bublé– *Crazy Love*
4 Black Eyed Peas – *The E.N.D. (The Energy Never Dies)*

5 Kings of Leon – *Only By The Night*
6 JLS – *JLS*
7 Beyoncé – *I Am . . . Sasha Fierce*
8 Paolo Nutini – *Sunny Side Up*
9 Lily Allen – *It's Not Me It's You*
10 Robbie Williams – *Reality Killed the Video Star*

Source: The Official Charts Company 2009

Susan Boyle's debut album has sold over 1.5 million copies in the UK. It sold more copies in the first week of release than any other album in chart history.

. . . Alcoholic Drinks (Brand)

1 Stella Artois   6 Smirnoff Red
2 Foster's   7 Hardy's
3 Carling   8 Strongbow
4 Blossom Hill   9 Budweiser
5 Carlsberg   10 Gallo

Source: Nielsen 2010

Launched in the late 1980s, Blossom Hill is the UK's best-selling wine; 25,000 glasses of Blossom Hill are consumed every hour.

Over half the cider drunk in the UK is Strongbow.

Gallo was started in 1933 by two brothers and is California's biggest exporter of wine.

. . . Alcoholic Drinks (Type)

1 Wine
2 Beer
3 Spirits
4 Cider

5 Sparkling wine
6 Champagne
7 Fortified wine
8 Alcopops

Source: Nielsen 2010

In 2009 sales of sparkling wine overtook champagne for the first time.

Sales of cider grew by 13% while sales of fortified wine fell by 6%.

Wine worth £5.2 billion was sold in the UK in 2009 compared with sales of alcopops, which were worth only £204 million.

. . . Alcopops

1 WKD
2 Smirnoff Ice
3 Bacardi Breezer
4 Caribbean Twist
5 Red Square

6 VK Vodka Kick
7 Gordon's Gin & Tonic
8 TVX
9 Greenall's Gin & Tonic
10 Pimm's & Lemonade

Source: Nielsen 2009

Sales of alcopops are still growing – by 2% in 2009.

526 hectolitres of alcopops were drunk in 2009.

TVX grew 16% in 2009 – more than any other brand. It is sold exclusively at Tesco.

. . . Ales

1 John Smith's Extra Smooth
2 Boddingtons
3 Old Speckled Hen
4 Newcastle Brown
5 John Smith's Original
6 McEwan's Export
7 Tetley's Smoothflow
8 Fuller's London Pride
9 Caffrey's
10 Tetley's Original
11 Hobgoblin
12 Marston's Pedigree
13 Abbot
14 Tanglefoot Bitter
15 Theakston's Old Peculier
16 Spitfire
17 Bombardier
18 Ruddles County
19 Greene King IPA
20 Bass

Source: Nielsen 2009

In 2009 sales of ale in shops (not pubs) were worth £475 million, up 7% on the previous year.

The largest percentage rise in the top 20 was for Marston's Pedigree, which grew by 30%.

The biggest fall was recorded by Caffrey's, selling 17% less in 2009.

. . . Alien Movies

1 *E.T. The Extra-Terrestrial*
2 *Men in Black*
3 *Independence Day*
4 *Alien*
5 *Transformers*
6 *Predator*
7 *Star Trek*
8 *War of the Worlds*
9 *The Fifth Element*
10 *Aliens*

Source: OnePoll 2009 for Phone Piggy Bank

Sales of Ray-Ban's Predator 2 sunglasses worn by Will Smith and Tommy Lee Jones in *Men in Black* tripled after the movie's release.

The Transformers toys were originally created by the Japanese company Takara and were called Diaclone and Microman.

On its release in 1997, *The Fifth Element* was the most expensive non-Hollywood film ever produced.

. . . Animated Movies

1 *Toy Story*
2 *Shrek*
3 *The Lion King*
4 *Finding Nemo*
5 *Ice Age*
6 *The Jungle Book*
7 *Monsters, Inc.*
8 *Beauty and the Beast*
9 *Bambi*
10 *Aladdin*
11 *Snow White and the Seven Dwarfs*
12 *101 Dalmatians*
13 *Who Framed Roger Rabbit?*
14 *Watership Down*
15 *Wall-E*
16 *Fantasia*
17 *The Nightmare before Christmas*
18 *The Little Mermaid*
19 *Cinderella*
20 *Alice in Wonderland*

Source: OnePoll 2009

Pixar's *Toy Story* was the first feature-length film to be made solely using CGI. Pixar started out as a company that sold high-end computers to the US government and the medical community before specialising in animation.

The first ever feature-length animated film was Walt Disney's *Snow White and the Seven Dwarfs*, released in 1937.

The only British entry in the top 20 is *Watership Down*, released in 1978. Based on a novel by Richard Adams, it is a mystical tale about rabbits finding a new home. The theme tune, 'Bright Eyes', was written by Mike Batt, better known as the man behind the Wombles pop band.

. . . Annoying Things

1 Chavs
2 People driving close behind you
3 People who smell
4 People who eat with their mouths open
5 Rude shop assistants
6 Foreign call centres
7 Stepping in dog poo
8 People who cough and do not cover their mouths
9 Slow Internet connections
10 Poor customer service
11 Dog owners who don't clean up after their dogs
12 Noisy eaters
13 Cold-callers
14 Door-to-door salesmen
15 Stubbing your toe
16 Bullying
17 Computer crashing, and losing work you've spent three hours doing
18 People who talk loudly on their mobile phones
19 Spam email
20 People's obsession with Z-list celebrities

21 Leaving a tissue in a pocket and putting the garment through the washing-machine
22 Driving slowly in the fast lane
23 Adverts in between programmes
24 Toilets you have to pay for
25 People's obsession with the Katie and Peter split saga
26 People reading over your shoulder
27 People who park in disabled bays when they're not disabled
28 Brown-nosers
29 People who complain about their weight yet make no effort to exercise or eat properly
30 People jumping the queue at the bar
31 Junk mail
32 Tailgaters
33 Big Brother
34 Muggers
35 MPs' expenses
36 Stepping in chewing-gum
37 Pricey train fares
38 People who walk painfully slowly on the street
39 Noisy neighbours
40 People who sniff and don't use a tissue
41 Sweating
42 The binge-drinking culture
43 Feeling bloated
44 The recession
45 Delays at the airport
46 Automated phone systems
47 Smoking

48 Road rage
49 People who have their mobile turned off when you really need to contact them
50 Running out of toilet roll
51 Coverage of Michael Jackson's death
52 Reality TV
53 Flies
54 Finding a flat tyre
55 Parking costs
56 Bossiness
57 Doctors' and dentists' inconvenient opening times
58 When your washing-machine breaks down
59 Politicians
60 Cutting yourself on paper
61 Buses not arriving on time
62 Singers who mime
63 People who can't park properly
64 Over-packaged kids' toys
65 Diarrhoea
66 Constipation
67 Text-message speak
68 Bad-hair days
69 Getting something in your eye
70 The hot water running out when you're running a bath
71 People who drive in the middle lane of motorways
72 People who mumble
73 Slow traffic lights
74 Cashiers giving you your change on top of the receipt

75 Cramp
76 Reading about the Brad Pitt/Jennifer Aniston saga
77 Unpredictable weather
78 Cars blocking pedestrian crossings
79 Adult acne
80 People who are not polite in emails
81 Yo-yo-dieting celebs
82 Trying to find the end of the Sellotape or toilet roll
83 Pimped-up cars
84 Traffic wardens
85 Losing your passport
86 Running out of petrol
87 Burning the toast
88 Sunburn
89 iPhone obsessives
90 Celebrity fitness DVDs
91 People addicted to watching soaps
92 Breaking a nail
93 Bankers
94 PDAs (public displays of affection)
95 Underperformance
96 Someone altering your seat height at work
97 People who don't remove their shoes in the house
98 Children at weddings
99 Hot weather when you're not on holiday
100 Sports commentary

Source: OnePoll 2009

The same poll was conducted a year earlier. We are becoming less worried about people reading over our shoulders – it was at number 5 in 2008 compared with number 26 in 2009. But we're more worried about stepping in dog poo, which was at number 19 in 2008, but in 2009 shot up to number 7.

The Nation's Favourite . . .

. . . BBC National Radio Stations

1 Radio 2

2 Radio 1

3 Radio 4

4 Radio 5 Live
  (inc. Sports Extra)

5 Radio 3

6 Radio 7

7 6 Music

8 1Xtra

9 Asian Network

Source: Rajar Q1 2010

BBC radio started in 1922 and was licensed by the government via the Post Office, because radio was seen as being related to electric telegraphs.

Radio 1 began broadcasting on 30 September 1967. The first record played was The Move's 'Flowers in the Rain'.

. . . BBC Regional Radio Stations

1 Radio Scotland

2 Radio Ulster

3 London 94.9

4 Radio Wales

5 Radio Merseyside

6 Radio Newcastle

7 Radio Solent

8 Radio Leeds

9 WM (Birmingham and the Black Country)
10 Radio Sheffield
11 Essex
12 Radio Lancashire
13 Sussex and Surrey
14 Radio Manchester
15 Radio Kent
16 Radio Devon
17 Radio Norfolk
18 Radio Humberside
19 Radio Leicester
20 Radio Nottingham
21 Radio Stoke
22 Radio Derby
23 Radio Bristol
24 Radio Cymru
25 Radio Cornwall
26 Tees
27 Three Counties Radio
28 Radio Berkshire
29 Radio Cumbria
30 Radio Suffolk
31 Radio Cambridgeshire
32 Radio Gloucestershire
33 Hereford and Worcester
34 Radio Lincolnshire
35 Radio Shropshire
36 Radio Northampton
37 Radio York
38 Coventry and Warwickshire
39 Radio Wiltshire

40 Somerset
41 Radio Jersey
42 Radio Solent
43 Radio Guernsey

Source: Rajar Q4 2009

The driving force behind setting up BBC local radio stations was a former war reporter called Frank Gillard. The first to air was Radio Leicester on 9 November 1967.

Radio Scotland has 864,000 listeners, while Radio Guernsey has just 18,000. Radio Guernsey, however, has a 25% share of the available audience while Radio Scotland can only manage 7.4%.

The most famous local radio presenter is fictional. Alan Partridge works for Radio Norwich hosting shows like *Up with the Partridge* and *Norfolk Nights*.

. . . Beatles Songs

1 'Hey Jude'
2 'In My Life'
3 'Strawberry Fields Forever'
4 'A Day In The Life'
5 'Yesterday'
6 'Eleanor Rigby'
7 'Let It Be'
8 'Penny Lane'

9 'Octopus's Garden'
10 'The Long And Winding Road'

Source: Daily Telegraph Readers' Poll 2003

'Hey Jude' was written by Paul McCartney for John Lennon's son Julian when his parents were getting divorced.

'Yesterday' was written by Paul McCartney when he was only 21. He claimed the melody came to him in a dream.

Strawberry Field was a Salvation Army children's home in Liverpool whose garden Lennon used to play in as a child.

. . . Beauty Products

1 Vaseline Lip Therapy
2 E45 Cream
3 Hair colorant
4 Nivea hand cream
5 Face wipes by Simple
6 Maybelline mascara
7 Johnson's Holiday Skin
8 Herbal Essences shampoo/conditioner
9 Olay moisturiser
10 Palmolive shower gel
11 Gillette razors
12 Frizz-Ease hair serum
13 Palmer's Cocoa Butter
14 Vaseline Intensive Care body moisturiser

15 Yves Saint Laurent Touche Éclat
16 Baby oil
17 St Ives Apricot Scrub
18 Nivea Aftersun
19 L'Oréal Elnett hairspray
20 Elizabeth Arden Eight Hour Cream

Source: OnePoll for Superdrug 2009

In the same survey 42% of people said they buy expensive brands as they look nicer on their bathroom shelves.

Vaseline is petroleum jelly, which was first discovered in 1859 as a by-product of the process of oil drilling in Titusville, Pennsylvania, then refined by a chemist called Robert Chesebrough. He opened the first Vaseline factory in 1870.

E45 Cream contains Medilan, which is derived from lanolin, the grease secreted by sheep that helps keep their wool waterproof.

. . . Bedtime Songs

1 Take That – 'Patience'
2 Robbie Williams – 'Angels'
3 Katy Perry – 'I Kissed a Girl'
4 James Blunt – 'You're Beautiful'
5 Elvis Presley – 'Love Me Tender'
6 Christina Aguilera – 'Beautiful'
7 Duffy – 'Warwick Avenue'

8   Guns N' Roses – 'Sweet Child O' Mine'
9   Oasis – 'Wonderwall'
10 Sugababes – 'Girls'

Source: OnePoll for TheBabyWebsite 2008

Two-thirds of mothers thought Take That's 'Patience' was more likely to send their child to sleep than a traditional lullaby.

Robbie Williams's 'Angels' is his most successful song, selling over 2 million copies worldwide.

Back to Bedlam, the James Blunt album that included 'You're Beautiful', was the bestselling UK album of the Noughties.

. . . Bedtime Stories

Julia Donaldson – *The Gruffalo*

Shortlist

Janet and Allan Ahlberg – *Each Peach Pear Plum*
Enid Blyton – *Five on a Treasure Island*
Eric Carle – *The Very Hungry Caterpillar*
Roald Dahl – *Charlie and the Chocolate Factory*
C.S. Lewis – *The Lion, the Witch and the Wardrobe*
A.A. Milne – *Winnie-the-Pooh*
Maurice Sendak – *Where the Wild Things Are*

Source: BBC 2009

The Gruffalo has sold 3.5 million copies and has been published in 31 foreign-language editions.

Published in 1942, *Five on a Treasure Island* was the first of 21 Famous Five adventures by Enid Blyton. The island in question is Kirrin, and the story begins when the children go to spend their summer holidays with their uncle and aunt at Kirrin Bay.

. . . Beers

1 Stella Artois
2 Foster's
3 Carling
4 Carlsberg
5 Budweiser
6 Carlsberg Export
7 Kronenbourg 1664
8 Beck's
9 John Smith's Extra Smooth
10 Tennent's
11 Guinness Draught
12 Stella Artois 4%
13 Grolsch
14 Carlsberg Special Brew
15 Peroni Nastro Azzurro
16 San Miguel
17 Corona Extra
18 Heineken
19 Boddingtons

20 Old Speckled Hen
21 Tennent's Super
22 Guinness Original
23 Cobra
24 Holsten Pils
25 Miller Genuine Draft
26 Newcastle Brown
27 Beck's Vier
28 John Smith's Original
29 McEwan's Export
30 Tetley's Smoothflow
31 Sol
32 Tiger
33 Coors
34 Leffe Blonde
35 London Pride
36 Tyskie
37 Skol
38 Murphy's
39 Caffrey's
40 Red Stripe
41 Brahma
42 Tetley's Original
43 Hobgoblin
44 Marston's
45 Tuborg
46 Skol Super
47 Castlemaine XXXX
48 Abbot
49 Tanglefoot Bitter
50 Budweiser Budvar

Source: Nielsen 2009

This list represents shop sales and does not include beer sold in pubs and restaurants. Shop sales here constitute 44% of the total beer market, but pub sales are falling and it is estimated that in 2010 more beer will be sold in shops than in bars.

1% less beer was sold in shops during 2009 than in 2008. This was due to a poor summer and increases on duty. Also, beer producers have been moving away from 18- and 24-packs to smaller sizes.

Stella Artois was the bestselling beer in 2008 too, but the number 2 beer, Foster's, has swapped places with Carling.

. . . Biscuits

1 McVitie's Chocolate Digestives
2 McVitie's Jaffa Cakes
3 Cadbury's Fingers
4 McVitie's Penguin
5 McVitie's Digestives

Source: TNS 2008

71 million packets of McVitie's Chocolate Digestives are eaten in the UK every year.

All the top 5 biscuits are over 50 years old. McVitie's Digestives were first made in 1892, McVitie's Chocolate Digestives in 1925 and Jaffa Cakes in 1927, McVitie's Penguin in 1932 and Cadbury's Fingers in 1957.

In 1991 McVitie's won a court case against the Inland Revenue, who wanted to charge VAT on Jaffa Cakes, claiming they were a biscuit not a cake (chocolate-covered biscuits are subject to VAT). McVitie's argued that biscuits go soft when they are stale whereas cakes, such as Jaffa Cakes, go hard.

One survey revealed 10.37 a.m. as the time office workers are most likely to have their first snack.

. . . Board Games

1 Monopoly	11 Backgammon
2 Scrabble	12 Connect 4
3 Trivial Pursuit	13 Operation
4 Chess	14 Ludo
5 Cluedo	15 Sorry!
6 Pictionary	16 Cranium
7 Snakes and Ladders	17 Risk
8 Game of Life	18 Battleships
9 Mah-jong	19 Draughts
10 Articulate	20 Solitaire

Source: OnePoll 2008

The highest single-word score ever recorded in Scrabble is 392 by Karl Khoshnaw for CAZIQUES. The highest opening word score is 126 by Jesse Inman for MUZJIKS (including a blank U).

Trivial Pursuit was invented in 1979 by a picture editor, Chris Haney, and a sports journalist, Scott Abbott. With the money he made from the game Abbott started his own ice-hockey team.

. . . Books We Pretend We Have Read

1 George Orwell – *1984*
2 Leo Tolstoy – *War and Peace*
3 James Joyce – *Ulysses*
4 The Bible
5 Gustave Flaubert – *Madame Bovary*
6 Stephen Hawking – *A Brief History of Time*
7 Salman Rushdie – *Midnight's Children*
8 Marcel Proust – *In Remembrance of Things Past*
9 Barack Obama – *Dreams from My Father*
10 Richard Dawkins – *The Selfish Gene*

Source: World Book Day 2009

Jonathan Douglas, Director of the National Literacy Trust, said, 'Research that we have done suggests that the reason people lied was to make themselves appear more sexually attractive.'

The same survey also asked people which authors they actually liked reading. J.K. Rowling came out top, John Grisham second and Sophie Kinsella third.

Almost half of the people surveyed said they had bought a book for someone else and read it themselves first.

. . . Boys' Names

1	Jack	29	Jayden
2	Oliver	30	Oscar
3	Thomas	31	Archie
4	Harry	32	Adam
5	Joshua	33	Riley
6	Alfie	34	Harvey
7	Charlie	35	Harrison
8	Daniel	36	Lucas
9	James	37	Muhammad
10	William	38	Henry
11	Samuel	39	Isaac
12	George	40	Leo
13	Joseph	41	Connor
14	Lewis	42	Edward
15	Ethan	43	Finley
16	Mohammed	44	Logan
17	Dylan	45	Noah
18	Benjamin	46	Cameron
19	Alexander	47	Alex
20	Jacob	48	Owen
21	Ryan	49	Rhys
22	Liam	50	Nathan
23	Jake	51	Jamie
24	Max	52	Michael
25	Luke	53	Mason
26	Tyler	54	Toby
27	Callum	55	Aaron
28	Matthew	56	Charles

57	Ben	79	Sam
58	Theo	80	Evan
59	Louis	81	Bradley
60	Freddie	82	Elliot
61	Finlay	83	John
62	Leon	84	Taylor
63	Harley	85	Joe
64	David	86	Corey
65	Mohammad	87	Reuben
66	Reece	88	Joel
67	Kian	89	Robert
68	Kai	90	Ellis
69	Kyle	91	Blake
70	Brandon	92	Aidan
71	Hayden	93	Louie
72	Zachary	94	Christopher
73	Kieran	95	Ewan
73	Luca	96	Jay
75	Ashton	97	Morgan
76	Bailey	98	Billy
77	Sebastian	99	Sean
78	Gabriel	100	Zak

Source: ONS 2009

There were 8,007 Jacks registered in England and Wales in 2008. It was the most popular boys' name during 2006–9.

The name growing most in popularity is Riley.

There were 26,815 different boys' names registered in the UK in 2008.

. . . Brands

1 Microsoft
2 Rolex
3 Google
4 British Airways
5 BBC
6 Mercedes-Benz
7 Coca-Cola
8 Lego
9 Apple
10 Encyclopædia Britannica Inc.

Source: Superbrands 2010

Microsoft was started on 4 April 1975 in Albuquerque, New Mexico.

Encyclopædia Britannica was first published in 1768 in Edinburgh, Scotland.

Over 2,000 Rolex watches are produced each day.

. . . Breakfast Cereals

1 Weetabix
2 Special K
3 Crunchy Nut
4 Kellogg's CornFlakes

5 Coco Pops
6 Cheerios
7 Rice Krispies
8 Oatso Simple
9 Shreddies
10 Frosties
11 All-Bran Flakes
12 Shredded Wheat
13 Alpen
14 Fruit 'n Fibre
15 Sugar Puffs
16 Dorset Cereals
17 Kellogg's Variety
18 Crunchy Nut Clusters
19 Weetos
20 Country Crisp

Source: Mintel 2009

Breakfast cereals have their origins in the nineteenth-century American vegetarian movement. They were developed as healthy foods that would cure complaints such as constipation. Early brands include Power, Vim, Vigor, Korn-Kinks and Climax.

Sales of Weetabix were worth £113 million in the UK during 2009, a rise of 7.9% on the previous year.

£286 millionworth of supermarket own-brand cereals are sold each year. The total market for breakfast cereals is £1,487 million.

. . . British Songwriters

1 Gary Barlow
2 John Lennon
3 Paul McCartney
4 Chris Martin
5 George Michael
6 The Bee Gees
7 Noel Gallagher
8 Robbie Williams
9 Sting
10 Kate Bush
11 Led Zeppelin
12 Guy Chambers
13 Paul Weller
14 Paul Simon
15 Morrissey
16 Bernie Taupin
17 Annie Lennox
18 David Bowie
19 Van Morrison
20 Cat Stevens

Source: OnePoll 2009

When still a teenager, Gary Barlow wrote a song called 'Let's Pray For Christmas' that reached the final of the BBC's magazine programme *Pebble Mill*'s 'Song for Christmas' competition.

The first song written by John Lennon and Paul McCartney was called 'Hello Little Girl' in 1957.

George Michael's first hit was with Wham!. 'Young Guns (Go For It)' was released in 1982 and was about a boy becoming too committed to a girl.

The Nation's Favourite . . .

. . . Cancelled Children's TV Shows

1 *Grange Hill*
2 *Thunderbirds*
3 *Live and Kicking*
4 *Fun House*
5 *Bagpuss*
6 *Record Breakers*
7 *Top Cat*
8 *DangerMouse*
9 *The Magic Roundabout*
10 *Rainbow*
11 *Mr Benn*
12 *The Wombles*
13 *He-Man and the Masters of the Universe*
14 *Byker Grove*
15 *Button Moon*
16 *Rosie and Jim*
17 *The Poddington Peas*
18 *The Raccoons*
19 *ThunderCats*
20 *The Animals of Farthing Wood*

Source: OnePoll 2010

Grange Hill was created by Phil Redmond (who also devised *Brookside* and *Hollyoaks*). The first episode was broadcast in 1978. The final episode aired on 15 September 2008.

32 50-minute episodes of *Thunderbirds* were made in 2 series. It was cancelled after Lew Grade failed to get an American network to show it.

Live and Kicking was broadcast from 1993 to 2001, and its most successful presenters were Zoë Ball and Jamie Theakston.

. . . Car Colours

1 Silver
2 Blue
3 Black
4 Red

Source: Motorparc/SMMT 2010

There were 31,035,791 cars on the road in the UK in 2009, a decrease of 0.7% on 2008 – the first time since the Second World War that the total had fallen and the first peacetime decline since 2006.

Silver has been the most popular car colour for the last two years – before this, blue held the top position.

. . . Car Sweets

1 Extra Strong Mints
2 Polos
3 Wine gums

4 Werther's Originals
5 Mint Imperials
6 Haribos

Source: Canvasse Opinion/Experian
for Post Office Car Insurance 2006

9 out of 10 drivers eat sweets on long car journeys.

Haribos are the number 1 choice for drivers under 35.

The favourite car sweet for women is Polos.

. . . Cars

1 Ford Fiesta
2 Ford Focus
3 Vauxhall Corsa
4 Vauxhall Astra
5 VW Golf
6 Peugeot 207
7 MINI
8 BMW 3 Series
9 Vauxhall Insignia
10 Ford Mondeo

Source: Motorparc/SMMT 2010

There were 1,994,999 new cars registered in 2009, a fall of 6.4% on the previous year (this followed an 11% fall in 2007).

117,000 Ford Fiestas were registered, 24,000 more than of the Ford Focus.

There were 34,418 Ford Mondeos registered.

. . . Cartoons

1 *The Simpsons*
2 *Tom and Jerry*
3 *South Park*
4 *Toy Story/Toy Story 2*
5 *Family Guy*
6 *Shrek/Shrek 2*
7 *The Lion King*
8 *Spirited Away*
9 *The Incredibles*
10 *Bugs Bunny*
11 *The Flintstones*
12 *The Iron Giant*
13 *The Nightmare before Christmas*
14 *Finding Nemo*
15 *Wallace and Gromit*
16 *Akira*
17 *Aladdin*
18 *The Ren and Stimpy Show*
19 *Who Framed Roger Rabbit?*
20 *Looney Tunes/Merrie Melodies*
21 *Princess Mononoke*
22 *Monsters, Inc.*

86 *Watership Down*
87 *Jamie and the Magic Torch*
88 *Woody Woodpecker*
89 *Felix the Cat*
90 *Captain Caveman and the Teen Angels*
91 *Mighty Mouse*
92 *Animal Farm*
93 *Mr Magoo*
94 *Queer Duck*
95 *Charley Says*
96 *Betty Boop*
97 *Huckleberry Hound*
98 *Wait Till Your Father Gets Home*
99 *The Pink Panther*
100 *Wacky Races*

Source: Channel 4 Poll 2004

The Simpsons started life as a series of short films that were shown on *The Tracey Ullman Show*, beginning on 19 April 1987. These then developed into a half-hour programme, which began broadcasting at the end of 1989. Over 450 episodes have now been made.

Tom and Jerry was created by William Hanna and Joseph Barbera in 1940. The extreme violence between Tom and Jerry is parodied in the cartoon *Itchy and Scratchy* that features in the Simpsons.

South Park tells the story of Stan, Kyle, Cartman and Kenny and is set in a fictional town in Colorado. It was first broadcast on 13 August 1997.

. . . Cats' Names

1 Tigger/Tiger	6 Harriet
2 Charlie	7 Poppy
3 Misty	8 Sam
4 Tom	9 Sooty
5 Smokey	10 Blackie

Source: MORI 2001

20% of people say that cats are their favourite type of animal.

1 in 50 cats is called Charlie.

5 of the top 10 cats' names are also common in humans.

. . . Champagnes

1 Moët & Chandon
2 Lanson
3 Veuve Clicquot
4 Heidsieck Monopole
5 Bollinger
6 Taittinger
7 Etienne Dumont
8 Piper-Heidsieck
9 Nicolas Feuillatte
10 Mumm

Source: Nielsen 2010

In 2010 Heidsieck Monopole increased sales in the UK by 79%.

136,000 hectolitres of champagne are drunk in the UK each year.

People in the UK spent £324 million on champagne in 2009. £39 is the average price of the bestselling brand, Moët & Chandon.

. . . Children's Films

1 *E.T. The Extra-Terrestrial*
2 *Toy Story*
3 *Mary Poppins*
4 *The Lion King*
5 *The Wizard of Oz*
6 *Bambi*
7 *Back to the Future*
8 *Shrek*
9 *Finding Nemo*
10 *Labyrinth*
11 *101 Dalmatians*
12 *Aladdin*
13 *Beauty and the Beast*
14 *The Goonies*
15 *The Jungle Book*
16 *Chitty Chitty Bang Bang*
17 *Alice in Wonderland*
18 *Home Alone*
19 *Ice Age*
20 *Harry Potter and the Philosopher's Stone*

21 *Snow White and the Seven Dwarfs*

22 *Annie*

23 *Cinderella*

24 *Monsters, Inc.*

25 *Madagascar*

26 *The Sound of Music*

27 *The Wrong Trousers* (Wallace and Gromit)

28 *Mrs Doubtfire*

29 *Babe*

30 *Beethoven*

31 *Beetlejuice*

32 *Black Beauty*

33 *The Little Mermaid*

34 *The Railway Children*

35 *A Bug's Life*

36 *Dumbo*

37 *Wall-E*

38 *The Lion, the Witch and the Wardrobe*

39 *A Little Princess*

40 *Bill and Ted's Excellent Adventure*

41 *Jurassic Park*

42 *Kung Fu Panda*

43 *Who Framed Roger Rabbit?*

44 *Billy Elliot*

45 *Lady and the Tramp*

46 *The Neverending Story*

47 *Short Circuit*

48 *Sleeping Beauty*

49 *An American Tail*

50 *Chicken Run*

Source: OnePoll 2010

Mary Poppins is based on a series of books by P.L. Travers. It was released by Walt Disney in 1964 and starred Julie Andrews and Dick Van Dyke. It is notable for its mixture of live action and animation (and Dick Van Dyke's cockney accent).

The Wizard of Oz was based on the 1900 novel *The Wonderful Wizard of Oz* by L. Frank Baum. It was released in 1939 and starred Judy Garland.

Labyrinth, released in 1986, was directed by master puppeteer Jim Henson and starred David Bowie as Jareth the Goblin King, a role for which he has been much mocked.

. . . Children's Films that Grown-ups Love

1 *Shrek*
2 *Pirates of the Caribbean: The Curse of the Black Pearl*
3 *Finding Nemo*
4 *Toy Story*
5 *Harry Potter and the Philosopher's Stone*
6 *The Lion King*
7 *Mrs Doubtfire*
8 *Monsters, Inc.*
9 *Ice Age*
10 *The Curse of the Were-Rabbit* (Wallace and Gromit)
11 *Madagascar*

12 *The Chronicles of Narnia*
13 *Wall-E*
14 *A Bug's Life*
15 *Matilda*
16 *Babe*
17 *Ratatouille*
18 *The Incredibles*
19 *Bambi*
20 *The Little Mermaid*

Source: OnePoll 2009

Shrek was based on a children's book written by William Steig and published in 1990.

Mrs Doubtfire was based on the young adults' novel *Madame Doubtfire*, written by Anne Fine and published in 1987.

'The Chronicles of Narnia' is a series of seven novels written by C. S. Lewis. The first book in the series, *The Lion, the Witch and the Wardrobe*, was published in 1950.

. . . Christmas Carols

1 'O Holy Night'
2 'Silent Night'
3 'Hark! The Herald Angels Sing'
4 'In the Bleak Midwinter' (music by Gustav Holst)

5 'In the Bleak Midwinter' (music by Harold Darke)
6 'O Little Town of Bethlehem'
7 'Once in Royal David's City'
8 'The Shepherds' Farewell' (music by Hector Berlioz)
9 'O Come, All Ye Faithful'
10 'It Came upon the Midnight Clear'

Source: Classic FM 2006

Placide Cappeau, the mayor of Roquemaure in France, wrote the words for 'O Holy Night' in 1847. The music was written by Adolphe Adam, a composer best known for his ballet *Giselle*.

'Hark! The Herald Angels Sing' was written by Charles Wesley, brother of the founder of Methodism, John Wesley. Originally the opening words were 'Hark! how all the welkin rings/ Glory to the King of Kings'. 'Welkin' means heaven.

Royal David was the second King of Israel, best known for slaying Goliath. His city was Bethlehem.

. . . Ciders

1 Strongbow
2 Magners
3 Bulmer's Original
4 Bulmer's Pear

5 Frosty Jack's

6 Jacques

7 Scrumpy Jack

8 Blackthorn

9 Gaymer's Olde English

10 Kopparberg Pear Cider (Sweden)

Source: Nielsen 2010

Gaymer's Olde English was first produced commercially in 1770 in Banham, Norfolk. There are records showing that Gaymer's had been producing cider since 1680.

Magners was developed to be sold via the international network of Irish pubs. In Ireland it is called Bulmer's Original Vintage. Internationally it is called Magners, to avoid confusion with the separate English-based H.P. Bulmer's company.

. . . Cigarettes

1 Lambert & Butler King Size

2 Mayfair King Size

3 Marlboro King Size Gold

4 Benson & Hedges Gold King Size

5 Richmond King Size

6 Richmond Superkings

7 Benson & Hedges Silver King Size

8 Silk Cut King Size Purple

9 Mayfair King Size Smooth

10 Royals King Size Red

11 Regal King Size
12 Superkings
13 Sterling Superkings
14 Embassy No. 1 King Size
15 Richmond Superkings Menthol
16 Lambert & Butler King Size Gold
17 Mayfair Superkings
18 Sterling King Size
19 Sovereign King Size
20 Silk Cut King Size Silver

Source: Nielsen 2010

Sales of Lambert & Butler cigarettes were worth £1.3 billion in 2009, a drop of 3% from the previous year.

The biggest rise in popularity was the super-value brand Sterling, which grew over 50% in 2009.

£5.85 is the average price for a packet of cigarettes – in 2000 it was £3.88 and in 1990 only £1.65.

The nation's favourite rolling tobacco is Golden Virginia.

. . . Classical Pieces

1 Georges Bizet – 'Au fond du temple saint' from *The Pearl Fishers* (1)
2 Edward Elgar – 'Nimrod' from *The Enigma Variations* (16)

3 Giuseppe Verdi – 'Va, pensiero' from *Nabucco* (22)

4 Max Bruch – Violin Concerto No. 1 in G Minor (12)

5 Johann Pachelbel – Canon in D Major (52)

6 Wolfgang Amadeus Mozart – Clarinet Concerto in A Major (33)

7 Ludwig van Beethoven – Symphony No. 6 in F Major (*Pastoral*) (27)

8 Sergei Rachmaninoff – Piano Concerto No. 2 in C Minor (8)

9 Pietro Mascagni – Intermezzo from *Cavalleria Rusticana* (23)

10 Ralph Vaughan Williams – 'Lark Ascending'

11 Jean Sibelius – *Finlandia* (2)

12 Ludwig van Beethoven – Symphony No. 9 in D Minor (*Choral*) (5)

13 Gustav Holst – *The Planets* (9)

14 George Frideric Handel – 'Ombra mai fù' from *Serse* (*Xerxes*) (17)

15 Wolfgang Amadeus Mozart – Piano Concerto No. 21 in C Major (25)

16 Samuel Barber – *Adagio for Strings* (14)

17 Ludwig van Beethoven – Piano Concerto No. 5 in E Flat Major (*Emperor*) (24)

18 Jules Massenet – 'Méditation' from *Thaïs* (39)

19 Antonín Dvořák – Symphony No. 9 in E Minor (*New World*) (36)

20 Ralph Vaughan Williams – *Fantasia on a Theme of Thomas Tallis*

21 Wolfgang Amadeus Mozart – 'Ave Verum Corpus' (28)

39 Felix Mendelssohn – Violin Concerto in E Minor (40)

40 Giacomo Puccini – 'Che gelida manina' from *La Bohème* (89)

41 Antonio Vivaldi – *The Four Seasons*

42 Ludwig van Beethoven – Symphony No. 5

43 César Franck – 'Panis Angelicus' (13)

44 Michael Balfe – 'I Dreamt I Dwelt in Marble Halls' from *The Bohemian Girl* (–)

45 Pyotr Tchaikovsky – Piano Concerto No. 1

46 Giuseppe Verdi – 'Grand March' from *Aïda* (26)

47 'Londonderry Air' – a traditional tune arranged by Percy Grainger (59)

48 Franz Lehár – *The Merry Widow* (67)

49 Giacomo Puccini – 'Nessun dorma' from *Turandot* (51)

50 Gabriel Fauré – *Cantique de Jean Racine*

51 Gabriel Fauré – 'In Paradisu' from *Requiem*

52 Ludwig van Beethoven – Symphony No. 7

53 Johann Sebastian Bach – Toccata and Fugue in D Minor

54 Albinoni – Adagio in G Minor

55 Charles Gounod – 'Judex' from *Mors et Vita*

56 Sergei Rachmaninoff – *Rhapsody on a Theme by Paganini*

57 Richard Addinsell – The Warsaw Concerto

58 Aram Khachaturian – Adagio from *Spartacus*

59 Pyotr Tchaikovsky – *Romeo and Juliet*

60 Carl Zeller – 'Don't Be Cross' from *The Foreman* (*Der Obersteiger*) (79)

61 Franz Schubert – 'Sanctus' from *The German Mass* (*Deutsche Messe*) (20)

62 George Frideric Handel – 'I Know That My Redeemer Liveth' from *The Messiah* (10)
63 Giacomo Puccini – 'Love Duet' from *Madame Butterfly* (15)
64 Ralph Greaves – Fantasia on 'Greensleeves' (based on *Sir John in Love* by Ralph Vaughan Williams)
65 Sergei Rachmaninoff – Symphony No. 2
66 Felix Mendelssohn – *Fingal's Cave*
67 Alexander Borodin – 'Polovtsian Dances' from *Prince Igor*
68 Gilbert and Sullivan – *The Yeomen of the Guard*
69 John Williams – *Schindler's List* theme
70 Gustav Mahler – Adagietto from Symphony No. 5
71 Charles Gounod – 'Sanctus' from *St Cecilia Mass*
72 Nikolai Rimsky-Korsakov – *Scheherazade*
73 Carl Teike – 'Old Comrades', march (11)
74 Wolfgang Amadeus Mozart – *The Marriage of Figaro*
75 Ralph Benatzky – *Casanova* (based on Johann Strauss II's 'Nuns' Chorus') (7)
76 Pyotr Tchaikovsky – *1812 Overture*
77 Hubert Parry – 'Jerusalem' (58)
78 Edvard Grieg – 'Morning Mood' from *Peer Gynt Suite No. 1* (47)
79 Joaquín Rodrigo – *Concierto de Aranjuez*
80 Christoph Gluck – 'Dance of the Blessed Spirits' from *Orfeo ed Euridice* (–)
81 Vincenzo Bellini – 'Casta diva' from *Norma*
82 Pyotr Tchaikovsky – *The Nutcracker Suite*

83 Camille Saint-Saëns – 'Softly Awakes My Heart' from *Samson and Delilah* (49)

84 Wolfgang Amadeus Mozart – *Eine Kleine Nachtmusik*

85 Franz Schubert – 'Ave Maria' (43)

86 Giacomo Puccini – 'O mio babbino caro' from *Gianni Schicchi*

87 Ludwig van Beethoven – *The Moonlight Sonata*

88 Johann Sebastian Bach – 'Sheep May Safely Graze'

89 Edward Elgar – 'Where Corals Lie' from *Sea Pictures*

90 Johann Sebastian Bach – Concerto for 2 Violins in D Minor

91 Claude Debussy – *Clair de Lune*

92 Joseph Haydn – *The Creation* (77)

93 William Walton – 'Crown Imperial', march

94 Oley Speaks – 'On the Road to Mandalay'

95 Ludwig van Beethoven – Romance No. 2 in F Major

96 Ronald Binge – 'The Watermill' (35)

97 Frederick Weatherly and Stephen Adams – 'The Holy City'

98 Graham Peel – 'Bredon Hill' from A.E. Housman's *A Shropshire Lad*

99 Gioacchino Rossini – 'William Tell Overture' from *William Tell*

100 Felix Mendelssohn – 'Hear My Prayer'

Source: BBC 2007

These are the results of the last poll conducted by the programme *Your Hundred Best Tunes*, broadcast on Radio 2 (and previously by the BBC Light Programme) from 1959 until 2007. The results of the show's previous poll in 1997 are shown in brackets.

The programme was presented by its creator, Alan Keith, who continued working on it until his death aged 94 in 2003.

'Londonderry Air', at number 47, was also the show's theme tune.

. . . Comedians

    1 Billy Connolly
    2 Victoria Wood
    3 Tommy Cooper
    4 Michael McIntyre
    5 Lee Evans
    6 Jimmy Carr
    7 Les Dawson
    8 Frank Skinner
    9 Jim Davidson
 10=Ricky Gervais
     Bill Bailey

Source: Ask Jeeves 2010

More than half the people asked in the survey thought modern comedians swore too much.

Tommy Cooper was bought his first magic set at the age of 8 and although his act consisted of tricks that went wrong he was a well respected magician as well as uniquely funny.

The fastest-selling stand-up-comedy DVD of all time is Michael McIntyre's *Hello Wembley!*.

. . . Comedy Songs

1 Monty Python – 'Always Look on the Bright Side of Life'
2 Benny Hill – 'Ernie, The Fastest Milkman in the West'
3 Monty Python – 'The Lumberjack Song'
4 The Wurzels – 'The Combine Harvester'
5 Rolf Harris – 'Jake the Peg'
6 Billy Connolly – 'D.I.V.O.R.C.E.'
7 Allan Sherman – 'Hello Muddah, Hello Faddah'
8 Victoria Wood – 'Let's Do It'
9 Spitting Image – 'The Chicken Song'
10 The Goons – 'The Ying Tong Song'
11 The Firm – 'Star Trekkin''
12 Chas & Dave – 'Rabbit'
13 Monty Python – 'Every Sperm Is Sacred'
14 Sophia Loren and Peter Sellers – 'Goodness Gracious Me'
15 The Goodies – 'Funky Gibbon'
16 *The Simpsons* (movie) – 'Spider Pig'
17 Andy Stewart – 'Donald Where's Your Troosers?'

18 South Park – 'Chef's Chocolate Salty Balls'
19 Cliff Richard & The Young Ones – 'Living Doll'
20=Terry Scott – 'My Brother'
    Tenacious D – 'Tribute'
    The Goons – 'I'm Walking Backwards for Christmas'

Source: YouGov 2009 for Reader's Digest

Under-34s picked 'Spider Pig' from *The Simpsons* movie as their top choice.

Under-24s picked 'Tribute' by Jack Black's rock group Tenacious D.

'D.I.V.O.R.C.E.' by Billy Connolly was the most popular in Scotland.

. . . Computer Games (all formats, in 2009)

1 *Call of Duty: Modern Warfare 2*
2 *FIFA 10*
3 *Wii Sports Resort*
4 *Wii Fit*
5 *Wii Fit Plus*
6 *Assassin's Creed II*
7 *Mario Kart Wii*
8 *Mario & Sonic at the Olympic Winter Games*

9   *Call Of Duty: World At War*

10 *FIFA 09*

11 *New Super Mario Bros. Wii*

12 *Wii Play*

13 *Professor Layton and the Curious Village*

14 *Forza Motorsport 3*

15 *Lego Batman: The Videogame*

16 *Call of Duty 4: Modern Warfare*

17 *Need for Speed: Shift*

18 *Resident Evil 5*

19 *Dr Kawashima's Brain Training*

20 *Mario & Sonic at the Olympic Games*

Source: ELSPA/GfK Chart-Track 2009

Call of Duty: Modern Warfare 2 sold 4.7 million copies in the first 24 hours after its release. By March 2010 it had sold 14 million copies worldwide. It is the second-bestselling game in the UK of all time, and third-bestselling game in the US of all time.

. . . Countries to Visit

1 Spain

2 France

3 USA

4 Irish Republic

5 Italy

6 Germany

7 Portugal
8 Greece
9 Netherlands
10 Turkey
11 Belgium
12 Poland
13 Cyprus

Source: ONS 2008

14 million people visit Spain each year and almost 11 million visit France – everywhere else has fewer than 5 million visitors.

There are over 400,000 Polish people living in the UK.

. . . Cracker Jokes

1 Doctor: What seems to be the problem?
   Santa: I seem to have a mince pie stuck up my bottom!
   Doctor: I've got just the cream for that!

2 Why did the scientist install a knocker on his door?
   He wanted to win the no-bell prize.

3 What goes oh, oh, oh?
   Santa walking backwards.

4 What do you call a bunch of chess grand-
   masters bragging about their games in a hotel
   lobby?
   Chess nuts boasting in an open foyer.

5 What did Adam yell on the day before
   Christmas?
   'It's Christmas, Eve!'

6 What do you call a penguin in the Sahara
   Desert?
   Lost.

7 What kind of room has no windows or doors?
   A mushroom.

8 What do you call a man with brown paper
   trousers?
   Russell.

9 How did the human cannonball lose his job?
   He got fired.

10 Why don't ducks tell jokes when they're flying?
   Because they would quack up.

Source: OnePoll for Mrs Christmas 2009

25 million boxes of crackers are sold every year.

Christmas crackers were invented by London sweetmaker
Thomas Smith, who used them to promote sweet sales.

. . . Cricket Commentators

1 Richie Benaud
2 Michael Holding
3 Geoffrey Boycott
4 David Gower
5 Mark Nicholas
6 Ian Botham
7 Mike Atherton
8 David Lloyd
9 Nasser Hussain
10 Simon Hughes

Source: The Wisden Cricketer/Cricinfo 2005

Richie Benaud got three times as many votes as Simon Hughes. He made his first broadcast for the BBC in 1960 and commentated on over 500 Test matches. His final commentary in the UK was in 2005.

Everyone in the top 10 played cricket professionally.

. . . Crisps

1 Walker's
2 Pringles
3 Doritos
4 McCoy's
5 Kettle Chips
6 Quavers
7 Hula Hoops
8 Sensations
9 Mini Cheddars
10 Wotsits

Source: Nielsen 2010

Walker's sold £498 millionworth of crisps in 2009, over £3 millionworth more than their nearest rival Pringles.

Doritos, with sales of £104 million, saw over 10% sales growth in 2008 and 2009 and are now only £36 million behind Pringles.

Pringles' distinctive can was invented by Fredric J. Baur. He died in 2008 and part of his cremated remains was buried in a Pringles container.

Over 16 billion Hula Hoops are eaten every year.

. . . Cuisines

1 Chinese	6 American
2 Indian	7 Mexican
3 British	8 Japanese
4 Italian	9 Greek
5 Thai	10 French

Source: OnePoll for Sharwoods 2010

39% of people chose Chinese food as their favourite.

Belfast is the city with the most exotic tastes. Each person there spends an average of £60 per month on foreign food.

People living in Aberdeen are the least keen on exotic food, spending just over £40 per month.

. . . Curries

1 Tikka masala
2 Korma
3 Rogan josh
4 Balti
5 Jalfrezi

6 Biryani
7 Madras
8 Bhuna
9 Dopiaza
10 Pasanda

Source: OnePoll for Patak's 2009

The region of the UK that curry is most popular in is Scotland.

Each month, the typical Brit will have three curries.

The Nation's Favourite . . .

. . . Daily Newspapers

1 *Sun*

2 *Daily Mail*

3 *Daily Mirror*

4 *Daily Star*

5 *Daily Telegraph*

6 *Daily Express*

7 *The Times*

8 *Financial Times*

9 *Daily Record*

10 *Guardian*

11 *Independent*

Source: ABC April 2010

The *Sun* sells just under 3 million copies every day, which are read by over seven and a half million people.

The *Daily Mail* was first published in 1896. The *Sun* was launched in 1963.

All daily newspaper sales are falling year on year.

. . . Dead Persons
We Would Like to Meet

1 Jesus

2 Princess Diana

3 William Shakespeare

4 Albert Einstein

5 Marilyn Monroe

6 Leonardo da Vinci

7 Elvis Presley

8 Roald Dahl
9 Freddie Mercury
10 Martin Luther King

Source: OnePoll for Primeval 3 2009

20% of people said they would like to visit Victorian Britain.

18% of people said they would like to visit Britain just after the Second World War.

10% said they would like to visit prehistoric Britain.

Jade Goody was 44th in the list, with 5.5% of the votes.

. . . Desert Island Tracks

1 Queen – 'Bohemian Rhapsody'
2 Robbie Williams – 'Angels'
3 Queen – 'Don't Stop Me Now'
4 Jeff Buckley – 'Hallelujah'
5 ABBA – 'Dancing Queen'
6 Michael Jackson – 'Billie Jean'
7 Elvis – 'Suspicious Minds'
8 Louis Armstrong –'Wonderful World'
9 Guns N' Roses – 'Sweet Child O' Mine'
10 Lady Gaga – 'Poker Face'

Source: PRS 2009

Robbie Williams was top of the poll for ideal male desert island companion.

Kylie Minogue was top of the poll for ideal female desert island companion.

The radio programme *Desert Island Discs* was launched in 1942 and is the second-longest-running radio show in the world.

. . . Designs

1 Concorde
2 London Underground map
3 Supermarine Spitfire aircraft
4 Mini
5 World Wide Web
6 Routemaster bus
7 Cat's-eye (road furniture)
8 *Tomb Raider* cover
9 *Grand Theft Auto* cover
10 K2 telephone kiosk

Source: Design Museum/BBC 2006 –
designs created after 1900

Concorde made its first flight from Toulouse in 1969.

The London Underground map was designed in 1931 by Harry Beck.

The Spitfire was designed by Reginald Mitchell in 1934.

. . . Diesel Cars

1 Ford Focus	6 Volkswagen Passat
2 Volkswagen Golf	7 BMW 3 Series
3 Ford Mondeo	8 Audi A3
4 Ford Fiesta	9 BMW 1 Series
5 Vauxhall Insignia	10 Audi A4

Source: Motorparc/SMMT 2010

832,456 diesel cars were sold in 2009 – almost half of all cars.

The bestselling diesel-powered car, the Ford Focus, sold 33,000. 60,000 non-diesel Focuses were also sold.

The first diesel car was the estate version of the Citroën Rosalie in 1933.

. . . Diets

1 Weight Watchers
2 Calorie Counting
3 Slimming World
4 Rosemary Conley
5 Kellogg's Special K

Source: OnePoll for Superdrug 2010

The average female spends 88 days a year on a diet – stopping and starting 4 times and sticking to each diet for 22 days.

41% of women decide to diet when their clothes stop fitting them.

The least favourite are the Cabbage Soup Diet, the Atkins Diet, the Grapefruit Diet, the Slim Fast and the Coconut Diet.

20% of women finish a diet and find they have put weight on.

. . . Dinner Dates

1 Stephen Fry
2 Cheryl Cole
3 Colin Firth
4 David Beckham

Source: Taste Of London 2010

Favourite families to dine with were the Osbournes followed by the Obamas, the royal family and the Beckhams.

The least favourite dinner date was Jordan followed by Michael Winner, Gordon Brown and Victoria Beckham.

. . . Dinners

1 Roast beef and Yorkshire pudding
2 Fish and chips
3 Chicken tikka masala
4 Steak and kidney pie
5 Spaghetti bolognaise
6 Bangers and mash
7 Lasagne
8 Shepherd's pie
9 Roast lamb
10 Creamy fish pie

Source: Somerfield

The earliest recipe for Yorkshire pudding dates back to 1737. It was devised as a way of cooking batter in the fat that drips off a joint of meat.

1 in 7 curries served in the UK is chicken tikka masala.

There is some argument over where the first fish and chip shop was opened. Both Joseph Malin's in the East End of London and Mr Lee's in Oldham opened around 1860.

. . . Dog Breeds

1 Labrador Retriever
2 Cocker Spaniel

3 English Springer Spaniel

4 German Shepherd Dog (Alsatian)

5 Cavalier King Charles Spaniel

6 Staffordshire Bull Terrier

7 Golden Retriever

8 Border Terrier

9 Boxer

10 West Highland White Terrier

11 Shih Tzu

12 Miniature Schnauzer

13 Lhasa Apso

14 Bulldog

15 Pug

16 Yorkshire Terrier

17 Whippet

18 Bull Terrier

19 Bichon Frisé

20 Rottweiler

Source: UK Kennel Club 2007/2008

Over 45,000 Labrador Retrievers were registered in 2008. These are also the most popular breed of dog in America and Canada. Although known as hunting dogs, they originate from the Newfoundland area of Canada, where they were used by fishermen to help drag their nets to shore.

The first German Shepherd, Horand von Grafrath, was registered in 1899. All modern German Shepherds can be traced back to this one dog.

The nation's favourite dog-food brand, Pedigree Chum, is owned by Mars, best known for its chocolate products. It was originally called Chappie and was first produced in Manchester in the 1930s.

. . . Dogs' Names

1 Ben	6 Toby
2 Max	7 Ellie
3 Bonnie	8 Meg
4 Sam	9 Poppy
5 Jack	10 Rosie

Source: MORI 2001

1 in 30 dogs is called Ben.

All the top 10 dogs' names are also used by humans.

On average, pet owners spend £7 a week on their pet. 1 in 20 spends more than £20 a week.

. . . Dunking Biscuits

1 Chocolate digestive
2 Rich tea
3 HobNob
4 Digestive
5 Chocolate Bourbon

6 Chocolate HobNob
7 Chocolate chip cookies
8 Custard creams
9 Shortbread
10 Gingernut

Source: OnePoll 2009

75% of people dunked a biscuit in the last seven days.

89% of people dunk at work.

Chocolate digestives can be dunked for 8 seconds, compared with only 4 seconds for gingernuts and HobNobs.

. . . DVDs in 2009 (all categories)

1 *Harry Potter and the Half-Blood Prince*
2 *Quantum of Solace*
3 *Twilight*
4 *Transformers: Revenge of the Fallen*
5 *Slumdog Millionaire*
6 *Madagascar: Escape 2 Africa*
7 Michael McIntyre – *Hello Wembley!*
8 *Angels & Demons*
9 *High School Musical 3: Senior Year*
10 *Ice Age 3: Dawn of the Dinosaurs*

Harry Potter and the Half-Blood Prince sold 2.25 million copies.

TV DVDs

1 *The Inbetweeners:* Series 1 and 2
2 *Gavin & Stacey:* Series 3
3 *Family Guy:* Season 8
4 *Gavin & Stacey:* Series 2
5 *Planet Earth:* The Complete Series

The Inbetweeners sold over 500,000 copies.

Music DVDs

1 Take That – *The Circus Live*
2 Michael Jackson – *Moonwalker*
3 Cliff Richard and The Shadows – *The Final Reunion*
4 The Killers – *Live from the Royal Albert Hall*
5 Il Divo – *An Evening With Il Divo: Live in Barcelona*

Take That's *The Circus Live* sold 570,000 copies.

Children's DVDs

1 *Madagascar: Escape 2 Africa*
2 *Ice Age 3: Dawn of the Dinosaurs*
3 *Merry Madagascar*
4 *Monsters vs Aliens*
5 *Ice Age 2: The Meltdown*

Madagascar: Escape 2 Africa sold 1.29 million copies.

Comedy DVDs

1 Michael McIntyre – *Hello Wembley!*
2 Jeremy Clarkson – *Duel*
3 Frankie Boyle – *Live*
4 Michael McIntyre – *Live & Laughing*
5 Lee Evans – *Access All Arenas*

Michael McIntyre's *Hello Wembley!* sold 1.28 million copies.

Sport and Fitness DVDs

1 Davina – *Super Body Workout*
2 *Pump It Up!: Aeroburn*
3 Coleen Nolan – *Disco Burn*
4 Claire Richards – *5 Step Fat Attack*
5 Danny Dyer – *Football Foul-Ups*

Davina's *Super Body Workout* sold 168,000 copies.

Blu–ray

1 *Transformers: Revenge of the Fallen*
2 *Star Trek*
3 *Quantum of Solace*
4 *The Dark Knight*
5 *Terminator Salvation*
6 *Harry Potter and the Half-Blood Prince*
7 *Inglourious Basterds*

8 *Watchmen*

9 *X-Men Origins: Wolverine*

10 *Planet Earth*: The Complete Series

Transformers: Revenge of the Fallen sold 228,000 copies.

Source: BVA/Official Chart Company 2009

The Nation's Favourite . . .

. . . Excuses Not to Have Sex

1 I'm too tired
2 I'm not in the mood
3 I've got a headache
4 I've got to get up in the morning
5 I'm preoccupied with work
6 I'm angry with you
7 I can hear one of the children
8 You need a shower
9 I've got a bad back
10 Too soon in our relationship

Source: OnePoll 2009

Men are more likely to make excuses not to have sex than women.

33% of men said they made excuses because they didn't fancy their partner any more.

20% of women said they made excuses because they didn't fancy their partner any more.

40% of women admitted pretending they were asleep. 50% of men did the same.

The Nation's Favourite . . .

. . . Family Films

1 *Pirates of the Caribbean: Dead Man's Chest*
2 *Peter Pan*
3 *Shrek*
4 *Pirates of the Caribbean: The Curse of the Black Pearl*
5 *Willy Wonka and the Chocolate Factory* (1971)
6 *Mary Poppins*
7 *The Wizard of Oz*
8 *Toy Story*
9 *Pirates of the Caribbean: At World's End*
10 *Free Willy*

Source: Admiral 2009

Pirates of the Caribbean is based on a theme park ride, which opened in 1967 in Disneyland, California. It was the last attraction that Walt Disney had a hand in designing.

The star of *Free Willy* was an orca (killer whale) named Keiko. After the film's success there was a campaign to get Keiko released from his home in an amusement park in Mexico City. He was eventually moved to a bigger pool in Oregon.

. . . Fat People

1 Dawn French
2 Fern Britton
3 Peter Kay
4 Chris Moyles
5 Johnny Vegas
6 Nigella Lawson
7 Jo Brand
8 Beth Ditto
9 Charlotte Church
10 Cheryl Fergison
11 Sharon Osbourne
12 Lisa Riley
13 Jennie McAlpine
14 Eamonn Holmes
15 Cliff Parisi
16 Lisa Tarbuck
17 Antony Worrall Thompson
18 Ann Widdecombe
19 James Corden
20 Ruth Jones

Source: OnePoll 2008

The average weight of women in the UK is 10 stone 3.5 lbs. The average weight in 1951 was 9 stone 10lbs.

In America the average weight for women is 11 stone 1.5lbs.

. . . Favourite-sounding Words

1 Nincompoop	11 Weekend
2 Love	12 Incandescent
3 Mum	13 Wicked
4 Discombobulated	14 Lovely
5 Excellent	15 Lush
6 Happy	16 Peace
7 Squishy	17 Cosy
8 Fabulous	18 Bed
9 Cool	19 Freedom
10 Onomatopoeia	20 Kiss

Source: Ubisoft Poll 2007

Susie Dent from the TV show *Countdown* identified the following new words in 2009: 'hashtag' (the # symbol as used on Twitter); 'staycation' (a holiday when you just stay at home); and 'freemiums' (a free service with paid-for extras).

The American *Merriam-Webster Dictionary* compiled a list of the commonest words entered into their online search but that weren't in their dictionary. The top 10 were:

1 confuzzled (adj.): confused and puzzled at the same time
2 ginormous (adj.): bigger than gigantic and bigger than enormous
3 woot! (interjection): an exclamation of joy or excitement
4 chillax (verb): chill out/relax, hang out with friends
5 cognitive displaysia (noun): the feeling you have before

you even leave the house that you are going to forget something and not remember it until you're on the highway

6 gription (noun): the purchase gained by friction: 'My car needs new tires because the old ones have lost their gription.'

7 phonecrastinate (verb): to put off answering the phone until caller ID displays the incoming name and number

8 slickery (adj.): having a surface that is wet and icy

9 snirt (noun): snow that is dirty, often seen by the side of roads and parking lots that have been plowed

10 lingweenie (noun): a person incapable of producing neo-logisms

. . . Films in 2009

1 *Harry Potter and the Half-Blood Prince*

2 *Avatar*

3 *Ice Age 3: Dawn of the Dinosaurs*

4 *Up*

5 *Slumdog Millionaire*

6 *The Twilight Saga: New Moon*

7 *Transformers: Revenge of the Fallen*

8 *The Hangover*

9 *Star Trek*

10 *Monsters vs Aliens*

11 *A Christmas Carol*

12 *Night at the Museum 2*

13 *2012*

14 *Angels & Demons*

15 *Bolt*

16 *X-Men Origins: Wolverine*

17　*Sherlock Holmes*
18　*Bruno*
19　*Marley & Me*
20　*Alvin and the Chipmunks 2: The Squeakquel*

Source: Nielsen EDI/UK Film Council 2010

Harry Potter and the Half-Blood Prince took just over £50 million at the box office in 2009. *Avatar* took £41 million.

Avatar is the highest-grossing film of all time.

. . . First Dance at Weddings

1　Lonestar – 'Amazed'
2　Aerosmith – 'Don't Want To Miss A Thing'
3　Shania Twain – 'From This Moment On'
4　Bryan Adams – '(Everything I do) I Do It For You'
5　Take That – 'Rule The World'

Source: PRS/Wedding TV 2009

3 of the top 5 appeared first on movie soundtracks: Aerosmith's 'Don't Want To Miss A Thing' in *Armageddon*; Bryan Adams's 'Everything I Do' in *Robin Hood: Prince of Thieves* and Take That's 'Rule the World' in *Stardust*.

The other 2 songs are Country and Western. Lonestar's power ballad 'Amazed' was in the UK charts for 22 consecutive weeks, although the highest it ever reached was number 22.

. . . Flowers

1 Roses	6 Freesias
2 Carnations	7 Alstroemerias
3 Chrysanthemums	8 Gladioli
4 Daffodils and narcissi	9 Orchids
5 Tulips	

Source: Flowers & Plants Association 2010

Of all the houses on sale in the UK at any time it is estimated that 200 will be called Rose Cottage.

The carnation is the emblem of Mother's Day.

. . . Fortified Wines

1 Buckfast Tonic Wine
2 Harvey's Bristol Cream
3 Martini
4 Croft Original Pale Cream Sherry
5 QC
6 Stone's Original Green Ginger Wine
7 Cockburn's Special Reserve Port
8 Taylor's First Estate Reserve Port
9 Taylor's LBV (Late Bottled Vintage)
10 Tudor Rose

Source: Nielsen 2010

£324 million was spent on fortified wines in the UK in 2009, exactly the same as for champagne.

People in the UK drink over 3 times as much fortified wine as they do champagne.

Buckfast Tonic Wine was first made by monks in the 1890s. In 2009 sales increased by 40%, to £31 million.

The Nation's Favourite . . .

. . . Garden Tools

1 Secateurs
2 Trowel
3 Fork
4 Spade
5 Lawn mower

Source: Gardener's World Survey 2009

Secateurs were invented in 1815 by a French nobleman and gardener called Bertrand de Moleville. He was also the head of the royal secret police.

The lawn mower was invented 15 years later by Edwin Beard Budding, from Stroud, Gloucestershire. It was an adaptation of a machine originally designed to shave the rough surface of the woollen cloth used to make Guardsmen's uniforms.

. . . Gay Icons

Male

1 Elton John
2 Freddie Mercury
3 Stephen Fry
4 George Michael
5 Oscar Wilde

6 Will Young
7 Alan Carr
8 Paul O'Grady
9 Boy George
10 David Beckham

Source: OnePoll 2009

Although Elton John admitted to being bisexual in 1976, he only publicly said he was gay after divorcing Renate Blauel in 1988.

Female

1 Judy Garland
2 Kylie Minogue
3 Madonna
4 Cher
5 Liza Minelli
6 Marilyn Monroe
7 Shirley Bassey
8 Lily Savage
9 Dusty Springfield
10 Barbra Streisand

Source: OnePoll 2009

The *Advocate* magazine has called Garland 'the Elvis of homosexuals'.

Foul-mouthed scouser Lily Savage is the creation of comedian Paul O'Grady. There is a tribute act called Lily Salvage.

. . . Girl Bands

1 Girls Aloud
2 The Spice Girls
3 The Supremes
4 The Bangles
5 The Sugababes

6 The Pussycat Dolls
7 Bananarama
8 Destiny's Child
9 All Saints
10 Eternal

Source: OnePoll 2008

Bananarama had top 10 singles in the UK and US top 10 hits. They sold 40 million records worldwide.

Girls Aloud have had 20 consecutive top 10 singles and 4 number 1s.

. . . Girls' Names

1 Olivia
2 Ruby
3 Emily
4 Grace
5 Jessica
6 Chloë
7 Sophie
8 Lily
9 Amelia
10 Evie
11 Mia
12 Ella

13 Charlotte
14 Lucy
15 Megan
16 Ellie
17 Isabelle
18 Isabella
19 Hannah
20 Katie
21 Ava
22 Holly
23 Summer
24 Millie

25	Daisy	56	Madison
26	Phoebe	57	Amelie
27	Freya	58	Isobel
28	Abigail	58	Paige
29	Poppy	60	Lacey
30	Erin	61	Sienna
31	Emma	62	Libby
32	Molly	63	Maisie
33	Imogen	64	Anna
34	Amy	65	Rebecca
35	Jasmine	66	Rosie
36	Isla	67	Tia
37	Scarlett	68	Layla
38	Leah	69	Maya
39	Sophia	70	Niamh
40	Elizabeth	71	Zara
41	Eva	72	Sarah
42	Brooke	73	Lexi
43	Matilda	74	Maddison
44	Caitlin	75	Alisha
45	Keira	76	Sofia
46	Alice	77	Skye
47	Lola	78	Nicole
48	Lilly	79	Lexie
49	Amber	80	Faith
50	Isabel	81	Martha
51	Lauren	82	Harriet
52	Georgia	83	Zoë
53	Gracie	84	Eve
54	Eleanor	85	Julia
55	Bethany	86	Aimée

87	Hollie	94	Florence
88	Lydia	95	Alicia
89	Evelyn	96	Abbie
90	Alexandra	97	Emilia
91	Maria	98	Courtney
92	Francesca	99	Maryam
93	Tilly	100	Esme

Source: ONS 2008

There were 708,711 births in England and Wales in 2008 and 34,043 different names registered.

Holly is the favourite name for girls born in December.

In 2007 Olivia was the third-favourite name. In 2008 there were 5,317 Olivias registered.

Lexi, rising 40 places from 2007 to number 73, was the highest climber within the top 100.

. . . Google Search Terms in 2009

1	Facebook	6	eBay
2	BBC	7	news
3	YouTube	8	Google
4	Hotmail	9	Yahoo
5	games	10	Bebo

Source: Google 2010

Google was founded by Larry Page and Sergey Brin in 1998. Its unofficial slogan is 'Don't be evil.'

Facebook was founded by Mark Zuckerberg. Initially membership was limited to students at Harvard University.

. . . Gossip Topics

For Men

1 Drunken friends
2 News
3 Old schoolfriends
4 Female work colleagues
5 The sexiest girl at work
6 Spreading rumours
7 Promotions
8 Sex
9 Salaries
10 The boss

For Women

1 Other women
2 News
3 Relationship problems
4 Other people's relationships
5 Sex
6 Friends' weight gain
7 Soap operas

8 Other women's boyfriends/husbands
9 Mother-in-law
10 Celebrities

Source: OnePoll 2009

31% of men thought gossipping with their partner was better than sex.

Over 50% of women discuss their private lives with their friends.

. . . Guitar Riffs

1 Guns N' Roses – 'Sweet Child O' Mine'
2 Eric Clapton – 'Layla'
3 Aerosmith – 'Walk This Way'
4 Michael Jackson – 'Beat It'
5 Motorhead – 'Ace of Spades'
6 Jimi Hendrix – 'Voodoo Child (Slight Return)'
7 Queen – 'Another One Bites the Dust'
8 Nirvana – 'Smells Like Teen Spirit'
9 Deep Purple – 'Smoke on the Water'
10 Green Day – 'American Idiot'
11 AC/DC – 'Back in Black'
12 Dire Straits – 'Money for Nothing'
13 Black Sabbath – 'Paranoid'
14 Metallica – 'Master of Puppets'
15 Jimi Hendrix – 'Crosstown Traffic'
16 Status Quo – 'Caroline'

17 Guns N' Roses – 'Better'
18 Lenny Kravitz – 'Are You Gonna Go My Way?'
19 Ozzy Osbourne – 'Crazy Train'
20 The Darkness – 'I Believe In A Thing Called Love'

Source: OnePoll 2009

Michael Jackson's 'Beat It' is the only entry in the top 20 that isn't a rock song.

In 2004 Eric Clapton's 'Layla' was ranked 27 in *Rolling Stone* magazine's '500 Greatest Songs of All Time'.

The Nation's Favourite . . .

. . . Honeymoon Destinations

Long-haul

1 USA
2 Barbados and the Caribbean
3 The Maldives
4 Mexico
5 Australia
6 New Zealand
7 Mauritius
8 Brazil
9 South Africa
10 North Africa

27% of long-haul honeymooners went to the USA, only 2% to North Africa.

Short-haul

1 Spain
2 France
3 Italy
4 Portugal
5 Ireland
6 Austria
7 Germany
8 Croatia
9 Bulgaria
10 Poland

26% of short-haul honeymooners went to Spain, 15% to France and 14% to Italy.

UK

1 London
2 Lake District
3 Scotland
4 Wales
5 Peak District
6 Edinburgh
7 Glasgow
8 Norfolk
9 Cardiff
10 Suffolk

Source: teletextholidays.co.uk 2008

16% of honeymooners who stayed in the UK went to London, 15% to the Lake District.

The average honeymoon cost £2,580, with an extra £922 spent while on holiday.

42% of people would prefer guests at their wedding to contribute towards the honeymoon rather than provide a traditional present.

11% had other family members on their honeymoon to help with childcare.

. . . Household Brands

1 Cadbury's	11 Bird's
2 Heinz	12 Marks & Spencer
3 Coca-Cola	13 Oxo
4 Fairy	14 HP
5 Walker's	15 Andrex
6 Bisto	16 McVitie's
7 Branston	17 Calpol
8 Hellmann's	18 PG Tips
9 Vaseline	19 Ribena
10 Kellogg's	20 Nescafé coffee

Source: OnePoll 2010

John Cadbury opened a grocer's shop in Birmingham in 1824. He was from a Quaker family and thought drinking-chocolate was a healthy alternative to alcohol.

Heinz was founded in 1869 in Pittsburgh, Pennsylvania. It opened an office in the UK in 1896 and its first UK factory in Peckham, South London, in 1905.

. . . Houseplants

1 Orchids	6 Begonias
2 Chrysanthemums	7 Azaleas
3 Spring bulbs	8 Peace lilies
4 Poinsettias	9 Cacti
5 Cyclamen	10 Spider plants

Source: Flowers & Plants Association 2010

There are over 20,000 species of orchid – more than double the number of bird species.

There are roughly 30 species of chrysanthemums.

. . . Hymns

1 'How Great Thou Art'
2 'Dear Lord and Father of Mankind' – tune: 'Repton'
3 'The Day Thou Gavest' – tune: 'St Clement'
4 'Be Thou My Vision' – tune: 'Slane'
5 'Love Divine, All Loves Excelling' – tune: 'Blaenwern'
6 'Be Still, for the Presence of the Lord' – tune: 'Be Still'
7 'Make Me a Channel'
8 'Guide Me, O Thou Great Redeemer' – tune: 'Cwm Rhondda'
9 'In Christ Alone'
10 'Shine, Jesus, Shine'

Source: Songs of Praise 2005

'How Great Thou Art' was based on a Swedish poem, 'O Store Gud', written in 1885. The melody is from an old Swedish folk song. It was popularised by Billy Graham in the 1950s.

In 1967 Elvis Presley won his first Grammy for an album of gospel songs entitled *How Great Thou Art*.

'Shine, Jesus, Shine', written in 1987 by Graham Kendrick, is the nation's favourite modern hymn. Damian Thompson, the former editor-in-chief of the *Catholic Herald*, called it 'the most loathed of all happy-clappy hymns'.

The Nation's Favourite . . .

. . . Inspirational Books

1 Harper Lee – *To Kill a Mockingbird*
2 The Bible
3 Dave Pelzer – *A Child Called It*
4 John Gray – *Men Are from Mars, Women Are from Venus*
5 Anne Frank – *The Diary of Anne Frank*
6 George Orwell – *1984*
7 Nelson Mandela – *A Long Walk to Freedom*
8 Alex Garland – *The Beach*
9 Audrey Niffenegger – *The Time Traveler's Wife*
10 J.D. Salinger – *The Catcher in the Rye*

Source: OnePoll 2009

Harper Lee's 1960 classic has sold over 30 million copies worldwide.

The Bible has been translated into 2,233 languages and has sold an estimated 2.5 billion copies since 1815.

. . . Internet Search Questions in 2009

1 What is Twitter?
2 Have I got swine flu?

3   Is Lady Gaga a man?

4   Who is Aleksandr Orlov?

5   Is Michael Jackson dead?

6   Where is my nearest Primark?

7   Who is the father of Heather's baby in *EastEnders*?

8   What is the Lisbon Treaty?

9   When will the recession end?

10 What is cervical cancer?

Source: Ask Jeeves 2009

'What is the identity of Stig from *Top Gear*?' was the most asked in 2008.

Aleksandr Orlov is the Russian meerkat that stars in comparethemarket.com TV ads. He is voiced by Simon Greenall, who starred in the TV series *I'm Alan Partridge* as Geordie hotel worker Michael.

. . . iPlayer Audio Programmes in 2009

1   *Test Match Special*, Fifth Ashes Test, day 2

2   *I'm Sorry I Haven't a Clue*, series 51, episode 1

3   *5 Live Sport*, Manchester United v Liverpool, 14 March

4   *The Chris Moyles Show*, Take That special, 6 July

5   Stephen Nolan (boxing coverage overrun), 7 November

6 *The Jo Whiley Show*, Jay-Z special, 18 September
7 *Fry's English Delight*, series 2, episode 1
8 Classic Serial: *The Complete Smiley*, episode 1
9 *The News Quiz*, series 69, episode 6
10 *Desert Island Discs*, Morrissey interviewed

*Source: BBC Best-performing episode per series/title,
1 January–13 December 2009*

Test Match Special began broadcasting in 1957. Its famous theme music is 'Soul Limbo' by Booker T. & the M.G.'s.

. . . iTunes Downloads in 2009

Singles

1 Black Eyed Peas – 'I Gotta Feeling'
2 Lady Gaga – 'Poker Face'
3 Lady Gaga/Colby O'Donis – 'Just Dance'
4 Black Eyed Peas – 'Boom Boom Pow'
5 Cheryl Cole – 'Fight for This Love'
6 La Roux – 'In for the Kill'
7 Tinchy Stryder – 'Number 1'
8 Alexandra Burke (feat. Flo Rida) – 'Bad Boys'
9 Lily Allen – 'The Fear'
10 Kings of Leon – 'Use Somebody'

Source: iTunes 2009

The number 1 iTunes single in the US was 'Boom Boom Pow' by the Black Eyed Peas, with 'Right Round' by Flo

Rida at number 2. 'Boom Boom Pow' is notable for its rap, 'I'm so three thousand and eight, you so two thousand and late.'

iTunes launched in 2001. The iTunes Store launched in 2003. 6 billion songs have been downloaded since then.

Albums

1 Kings of Leon − *Only by the Night*
2 Lily Allen − *It's Not Me, It's You*
3 Lady Gaga − *The Fame*
4 The Prodigy − *Invaders Must Die*
5 Florence and the Machine − *Lungs*
6 Beyoncé − *I Am . . . Sasha Fierce*
7 Kasabian − *West Ryder Pauper Lunatic Asylum*
8 Michael Jackson − *Number Ones*
9 Black Eyed Peas − *The E.N.D. (The Energy Never Dies)*
10 The Script − *The Script*

Source: iTunes 2009

The US top 10 also had Kings of Leon at number 1 but had the soundtrack to the film *Twilight* at number 2.

70% of all digital downloads come from the iTunes shop.

... iTunes Movie Downloads in 2009

1 *Quantum of Solace*
2 *Yes Man*
3 *Watchmen*
4 *Role Models*
5 *Slumdog Millionaire*

6 *Marley & Me*
7 *Gran Torino*
8 *Star Trek*
9 *RocknRolla*
10 *Angels & Demons*

Source: iTunes 2009

'Quantum of Solace' is the title of an Ian Fleming short story, but the film contains no elements from it.

The Nation's Favourite . . .

. . . Karaoke Songs

1 ABBA – 'Waterloo'
2 Queen – 'Bohemian Rhapsody'
3 Frank Sinatra – 'My Way'
4 Gloria Gaynor – 'I Will Survive'
5 ABBA – 'Dancing Queen'
6 Robbie Williams – 'Angels'
7 Madonna – 'Like a Virgin'
9 Olivia Newton John and John Travolta – 'Summer Nights'
10 Kylie Minogue – 'I Should Be So Lucky'

Source: PRS 2009

In 2005 'Angels' topped a poll of songs people would most like played at their funeral. 'My Way' was number 2.

'Bohemian Rhapsody' is the third-bestselling UK single of all time. Number 2 is Band Aid's 'Do They Know It's Christmas?' and number 1 Elton John's 'Candle in the Wind' (1997).

The Nation's Favourite . . .

. . . Landmarks

1 Big Ben
2 Stonehenge
3 The white cliffs of Dover
4 Edinburgh Castle
5 London Eye
6 St Paul's Cathedral
7 Buckingham Palace
8 Tower Bridge
9 Houses of Parliament
10 The Roman baths in Bath

Source: OnePoll/Beautiful Britain 2010

70% of people say they love the British countryside.

80% of people think Britain is beautiful.

. . . Leisure Activities

Men

1 Watching television
2 Spending time with family and friends
3 Sport and exercise
4 Cultural activities
5 Shopping

6 Internet
7 DIY
8 Computer games
9 Arts and crafts

Women

1 Watching television
2 Spending time with family and friends
3 Shopping
4 Cultural activities
5 Sport and exercise
6 Internet
7 Computer games
8 DIY
9 Arts and crafts

*Source: Taking Part: The National Survey of Culture,
Leisure and Sport, Department for Culture, Media
and Sport, 2006/7*

These results come from an extensive government survey that is now almost 4 years old. It is estimated that Internet usage has increased by 65% since then.

Social network sites account for 22% of the time people spend online.

. . . Library Books in 2009

1 James Patterson – *Sail*
2 Linwood Barclay – *No Time for Goodbye*
3 James Patterson with Maxine Paetro – *7th Heaven*
4 James Patterson and Howard Roughan – *You've Been Warned*
5 Sadie Jones – *The Outcast*
6 Lee Child – *Nothing to Lose*
7 Patricia Cornwell – *The Front*
8 Harlan Coben – *Hold Tight*
9 John Grisham – *The Appeal*
10 Joanna Trollope – *Friday Nights*
11 Kate Morton – *The House at Riverton*
12 Francesca Simon – *Horrid Henry and the Football Fiend*
13 Ian Rankin – *Exit Music*
14 James Patterson and Michael Ledwidge – *The Quickie*
15 Ian Rankin – *Doors Open*
16 Danielle Steel – *Rogue*
17 Kathy Reichs – *Devil Bones*
18 Margaret Cezair-Thompson – *The Pirate's Daughter*
19 Julia Gregson – *East of the Sun*
20 Khaled Hosseini – *A Thousand Splendid Suns*
21 Maeve Binchy – *This Year It Will Be Different*
22 Patricia Cornwell – *Book of the Dead*
23 Karin Slaughter – *Fractured*
24 James Patterson – *Cross Country*
25 Maeve Binchy – *Heart and Soul*

26 Josephine Cox – *Songbird*
27 James Patterson – *Double Cross*
28 Jack Higgins – *Rough Justice*
29 Francesca Simon – *Horrid Henry and the Abominable Snowman*
30 James Patterson and Maxine Paetro – *The 6th Target*
31 John Hart – *Down River*
32 P.D. James – *The Private Patient*
33 Tess Gerritsen – *The Bone Garden*
34 Claire Freedman and Ben Cort – *Aliens Love Underpants!*
35 Michael Connelly – *The Overlook*
36 Jeffery Deaver – *The Broken Window*
37 Victoria Hislop – *The Island*
38 Val McDermid – *A Darker Domain*
39 James Bradley – *The Resurrectionist*
40 Robert Goddard – *Found Wanting*
41 Jacqueline Wilson – *My Sister Jodie*
42 James Patterson and Gabrielle Charbonnet – *Sundays at Tiffany's*
43 James Patterson with Michael Ledwidge – *Step on a Crack*
44 Michael Connelly – *The Brass Verdict*
45 Reginald Hill – *A Cure for All Diseases*
46 Danielle Steel – *Honour Thyself*
47 Katie Fforde – *Wedding Season*
48 Patrick Gale – *Notes from an Exhibition*
49 Marian Keyes – *This Charming Man*
50 Jonathan Kellerman – *Compulsion*

Source: Public Lending Right July 2008–June 2009

All the books in the top 50 are fiction.

James Patterson has written 55 bestsellers. He often works with a co-author.

Over the last ten years Jacqueline Wilson has been the most borrowed author (16 million loans) and her novel *The Story of Tracy Beaker* is the most borrowed book.

. . . Little Pleasures

1 A good night's sleep
2 Finding a forgotten tenner in your pocket
3 Cuddling up with a partner in bed
4 Crying with laughter
5 Having a lie-in
6 Sleeping in newly laundered bedding
7 Getting a bargain
8 Making someone smile
9 Catching up with an old friend
10 Laughing at things that have happened in the past
11 Eating a Sunday roast with your family
12 Someone saying you look nice
13 Curling up on the sofa with a good book and a hot drink or soup
14 Discovering you've lost a few pounds
15 Breakfast in bed
16 Waking up thinking it's a work day and then realising it's the weekend

17 A random person smiling at you in the street
18 Looking through old photo albums
19 Eating a takeaway
20 First snowfall of the year
21 Singing your heart out to your favourite song in the car
22 Having lunch with friends
23 Listening to a baby laughing
24 Having a massage
25 Reading a book or listening to your iPod on holiday by the pool
26 Playing in snow
27 Finding a pair of jeans that fit perfectly
28 Being chatted up
29 A girly night in
30 A pampering session at home
31 The smell of freshly cut grass
32 Sitting in the pub with your friends
33 Looking at a baby asleep in a cot
34 Waking up in a room with an amazing view
35 Clothes shopping
36 Receiving a letter from a friend
37 Fitting into an old pair of jeans again after losing some weight
38 Staying up all night getting to know someone special
39 Your mum's cooking
40 Getting dressed up for a night out
41 Watching a live band
42 Drinking a cold beer after work
43 Browsing in a secondhand bookshop

44 Going to the cinema
45 Getting a new hairstyle
46 Finding yourself in the quickest queue in the supermarket
47 The cold side of the pillow
48 Watching a DVD
49 Getting tipsy
50 Popping bubble-wrap

Source: OnePoll for Batchelors Cup-a-Soup 2009

The longest anyone has gone without sleep is 11 days. 17-year-old Randy Gardner achieved this feat in 1964.

. . . Love Songs

1 Bryan Adams – '(Everything I Do) I Do It For You'
2 Bon Jovi – 'Always'
3 Whitney Houston – 'I Will Always Love You'
4 Aerosmith – 'I Don't Wanna Miss a Thing'
5 Celine Dion – 'My Heart Will Go On'
6 Sinead O'Connor – 'Nothing Compares 2 U'
7 Elton John – 'Your Song'
8 Righteous Brothers – 'Unchained Melody'
9 Bonnie Tyler – 'Total Eclipse of the Heart'
10 Bee Gees – 'How Deep Is Your Love'
11 Cyndi Lauper – 'Time After Time'
12 U2 – 'All I Want Is You'
13 Celine Dion – 'Because You Loved Me'

14 Goo Goo Dolls – 'Iris'
15 Lionel Richie and Diana Ross – 'Endless Love'
16 Bryan Adams – 'Heaven'
17 Bryan Adams – 'Please Forgive Me'
18 Lonestar – 'Amazed'
19 Chris De Burgh – 'The Lady in Red'
20 Savage Garden – 'Truly Madly Deeply'

Source: OnePoll 2008

Bryan Adams's '(Everything I Do) I Do It For You' spent 16 weeks at number 1 in 1991, selling over 1.5 million copies.

Released in 1994, the power ballad 'Always' is Bon Jovi's biggest ever hit.

. . . Love Stories

1 Emily Brontë – *Wuthering Heights*
2 Jane Austen – *Pride and Prejudice*
3 William Shakespeare – *Romeo and Juliet*
4 Charlotte Brontë – *Jane Eyre*
5 Margaret Mitchell – *Gone with the Wind*
6 Michael Ondaatje – *The English Patient*
7 Daphne du Maurier – *Rebecca*
8 Boris Pasternak – *Doctor Zhivago*
9 D.H. Lawrence – *Lady Chatterley's Lover*
10 Thomas Hardy – *Far from the Madding Crowd*
11=Alan Jay Lerner – *My Fair Lady*
      C.S. Forester – *The African Queen*

13 F. Scott Fitzgerald – *The Great Gatsby*
14 Jane Austen – *Sense and Sensibility*
15=Arthur Laurents – *The Way We Were*
    Leo Tolstoy – *War and Peace*
17 Daphne du Maurier – *Frenchman's Creek*
18 Jane Austen – *Persuasion*
19 Kingsley Amis – *Take a Girl Like You*
20 George Eliot – *Daniel Deronda*

Source: UKTV Poll 2007

40% of women read romantic novels so as to feel better.

When publishing *Wuthering Heights* and *Jane Eyre* Emily and Charlotte Brontë used the pseudonyms Ellis and Currer Bell because they didn't want to reveal they were women.

Arthur Laurents also wrote the book (i.e. the words, not the music) for *West Side Story*, *Gypsy* and *La Cage Aux Folles*.

Kingsley Amis famously wrote, 'Sex is a momentary itch, love never lets you go.'

. . . Lyrics

1 John Lennon – 'Imagine' (Lennon)
2 Robbie Williams – 'Angels' (Williams and Chambers)
3 Queen – 'Bohemian Rhapsody' (Mercury)
4 The Beatles – 'I Am The Walrus' (Lennon and McCartney)

5 Robbie Williams – 'Millennium' (Williams, Chambers and Barry)

6 The Beatles – 'Yesterday' (Lennon and McCartney)

7 John Otway – 'Beware Of The Flowers' (Otway)

8 James – 'Sit Down' (Booth/Glennie/ Whelan/Gott)

9 Moody Blues – 'Nights In White Satin' (Moody Blues/ Hayward)

10 Hoagy Carmichael – 'Stardust' (Carmichael/ Parish)

Source: BBC 1999

John Otway's appearance at number 7 in the list was part of an orchestrated campaign by his followers.

'Nights In White Satin' was turned into a theme-park ride at the Hard Rock Park in South Carolina. The Moody Blues recorded a special version of the song to match the duration of the ride.

The Nation's Favourite . . .

. . . Magazines

1 *TV Choice*
2 *What's on TV*
3 *Radio Times*
4 *Take a Break*
5 *Saga Magazine*
6 *New!*
7 *Closer*
8 *OK! Magazine*
9 *Star*
10 *Glamour*
11 *Heat*
12 *Reader's Digest*
13 *Chat*
14 *Good Housekeeping*
15 *Now*
16 *That's Life*
17 *Cosmopolitan*
19 *Sainsbury's Magazine*
20 *Good Food* (BBC)
21 *Reveal*
22 *TV Times*
23 *National Geographic*
24 *Pick Me Up*
25 *Woman's Weekly*
26 *Woman*
27 *Look*
28 *Slimming World*

29 *Best*

30 *Woman's Own*

31 *Prima*

32 *People's Friend*

33 *Love It!*

34 *Yours*

35 *Candis*

36 *Bella*

37 *HELLO!*

38 *Company*

39 *Marie Claire*

40 *Grazia*

41 *Red*

42 *Men's Health*

43 *Gardeners' World* (BBC)

44 *Real People*

45 *Weight Watchers Magazine*

46 *Private Eye*

47 *FHM*

48 *TV & Satellite Week*

49 *Ideal Home*

50 *More!*

51 *TV Easy*

52 *Full House*

53 *Inside Soap*

54 *Empire*

55 *Nuts*

56 *Country Living*

57 *Top Gear Magazine* (BBC)

58 *House Beautiful*

59 *Computeractive*

60 *Puzzler Collection*

61 *Vogue*

62 *Elle* (UK)

63 *Easy Living*

64 *Economist* (UK)

65 *The Week*

66 *Healthy*

67 *My Weekly*

68 *Sugar*

69 *She*

70 *BM*

71 *Take A Crossword*

72 *InStyle* (UK)

73 *Your Home*

74 *TV Quick*

75 *Motor Cycle News*

76 *Essentials*

77 *Ideal Home Complete Guide to Christmas*

78 *Total TV Guide*

79 *Psychologies*

80 *Top of the Pops*

82 *The Simpsons Comics Magazine*

83 *Soaplife*

84 *Zoo*

85 *delicious*

86 *All About Soap*

87 *Time Magazine* (UK)

88 *Take a Puzzle*

89 *Runner's World*

90 *25 Beautiful Homes*

91 *Zest*

92 *Homes and Gardens*

93 *Puzzler*

94 *Stuff*

95 *New Scientist* (worldwide except Australia and US/Canada)

96 *Bliss*

97 *FourFourTwo*

98 *GQ*

99 *What Car?*

100 *Word Search*

Source: ABC second half of 2009

TV Choice sells 1.3 million copies compared with the *Radio Times*, which sells 1 million.

What's on TV was launched in 1991 when the monopoly on TV listings ended. Before then, viewers had to buy the *Radio Times* to find out about BBC programmes and *TV Times* for ITV.

. . . Men's Magazines

1 *Shortlist*

2 *Sport*

3 *Men's Health*

4 *FHM*

5 *Nuts*

6 *GQ*

7 *Zoo*

8 *Stuff*

9 *BBC Focus*

10 *Loaded*

11 *Men's Fitness*

12 *Esquire*

13 *T3*

14 *Healthy for Men*

15 *Wired*

16 *Front*

17 *Bizarre*

Source: ABC second half of 2009

Shortlist and *Sport* are both given away free.

Men's Health grew by 0.2% to be the highest-selling paid-for magazine.

Nuts' circulation has dropped almost 25% year on year. Its rival *Zoo* has fallen almost 30%.

. . . Michael Jackson Songs

1 'Thriller'

2 'Billie Jean'

3 'Beat It'

4 'You Rock My World'

5 'Man In The Mirror'

6 'The Way You Make Me Feel'

7 'Smooth Criminal'

8 'Bad'
9 'Black or White'
10 'Don't Stop Till You Get Enough'

Source: PRS 2009

'Thriller' was written by UK-born musician Rod Temperton, who also penned Jackson's hit 'Rock With You' and the disco classic 'Boogie Nights'.

91 versions of 'Billie Jean' were mixed before the final version was ready.

. . . Mobile Phones

1 Apple iPhone
2 Nokia 3210
3 Nokia 6310
4 Nokia 5100 range
5 Motorola RAZR V3
6 BlackBerry Curve 8300
7 Motorola 8000 range
8 Nokia 9000
9 Motorola MicroTAC
10 Nokia 7110

Source: University of Salford 2010

The Apple iPhone received 13.5% of the vote.

5 of the top 10 are made by Nokia, 3 by Motorola.

The world's first clamshell phone, Motorola's StarTAC, was number 12.

. . . Moustache-wearing British Men

1 Freddie Mercury
2 John Cleese
3 Lord Kitchener
4 Charlie Chaplin
5 David Seaman
6 Bruce Forsyth
7 Terry-Thomas
8 Peter Sellers
9 Des Lynam
10 Daley Thompson

Source: OnePoll for Remington 2009

Lord Kitchener sported a classic handlebar moustache, which was popular in Europe from the 1700s to about 1920.

Charlie Chaplin's toothbrush moustache became popular with the working class in the 1920s as a response to the type of moustache worn by people like Lord Kitchener.

... Museums

1 British Museum
2 Tate Modern
3 National Gallery
4 Natural History Museum
5 Science Museum
6 Tower of London
7 Victoria and Albert Museum
8 National Maritime Museum
9 National Portrait Gallery
10 Tate Britain

Source: ALVA 2008

The British Museum had 4.8 million visitors in 2008.

Kelvingrove Art Gallery and Museum in Glasgow was the most popular museum outside London.

More people visit Kew Gardens in London than the Eden Project in Cornwall.

Chester Zoo is more popular than London Zoo.

... Music Festivals

Major festival — Glastonbury
Medium-sized festival — Bestival
Small festival — Beach Break Live

Family festival – Camp Bestival
Dance music festival – Creamfields
Festival toilets – T in the Park
Headline performance – Blur at Glastonbury
Festival anthem of the year – Kings of Leon, 'Sex
   On Fire'

Source: Festival Awards 2009 voted by the public

180,000 people attend Glastonbury each year. It takes place during the last weekend in June. 2010 was its fortieth anniversary.

The world's biggest festival is Summerfest, which takes place in Milwaukee. Up to a million people watch performances from over 700 bands over the course of 11 days.

. . . Music Magazines

1 *Mojo*
2 *Q*
3 *Uncut*
4 *Classic Rock*
5 *Metal Hammer*
6 *Kerrang!*
7 *New Musical Express*
8 *The Word*
9 *Mixmag*
10 *BBC Music Magazine*
11 *Classic FM Magazine*

12 *Gramophone*
13 *Terrorizer*
14 *Rhythm*

Source: *ABC 2010*

Mojo sells 98,000 compared with *Q*'s 95,000.

Rock magazine *Kerrang!* is the bestselling weekly on 41,000 sales, compared with the *NME*'s 38,000.

Terrorizer specialises in covering the death metal scene.

. . . Musical Films

1 *Grease*
2 *The Sound of Music*
3 *The Wizard of Oz*
4 *West Side Story*
5 *Mary Poppins*
6 *Singin' in the Rain*
7 *Rocky Horror Picture Show*
8 *Chicago*
9 *Oliver*
10 *Moulin Rouge*

Source: *Channel 4 2003*

Grease was released in 1978. It took $340 million worldwide.

Julie Andrews starred in two of the top 5 films – *The Sound of Music* and *Mary Poppins*.

Outside the top 10, a surprise entry was the film *8 Mile*, starring Eminem.

. . . Musicals

1 *Les Misérables*
2 *The Phantom of the Opera*
3 *Seven Brides for Seven Brothers*
4 *The King and I*
5 *Sunset Boulevard*
6 *Evita*
7 *Chess*
8 *The Rocky Horror Show*
9 *Follies*
10 *Hair*

Source: BBC Radio 2 2005

Les Misérables received 41% of all votes cast.

4 of the top 10 were produced by Andrew Lloyd Webber.

The Nation's Favourite . . .

. . . National Treasures

1 William Shakespeare
2 Buckingham Palace
3 Fish and chips
4 Big Ben
5 Red telephone boxes
6 The cup of tea
7 Beatles
8 Red buses
9 The Queen
10 Stonehenge
11 London Bridge
12 Charles Dickens
13 Black cabs
14 Cadbury's chocolate
15 The Beatles
16 Wimbledon
17 Pubs
18 Westminster Abbey
19 St Paul's Cathedral
20 A roast beef dinner
21 Winston Churchill
22 A cream tea
23 Mini
24 Strawberries and cream
25 Edinburgh Castle
26 Cricket
27 The Glastonbury Festival

28 The Oxford and Cambridge boat race
29 Harrods
30 The royal family
31 Marks & Spencer
32 Ant & Dec
33 *Coronation Street*
34 The Rolls-Royce
35 The NHS
36 Bangers and mash
37 David Attenborough
38 The Grand National
39 Great Ormond Street Hospital
40 Royal Ascot
41 Judy Dench
42 Hampton Court
43 Lords Cricket Ground
44 Anthony Hopkins
45 Stephen Fry
46 Wembley Stadium
47 Fry-ups
48 J.K. Rowling
49 The Bentley
50 Concorde

Source: OnePoll for Mivvi 2009

The red telephone box was designed by Sir Giles Gilbert Scott and introduced in 1926.

Many black cabs have a turning circle of only 25 feet, which is based on the size of the small roundabout in front of the Savoy Hotel.

... *Neighbours* Characters

1 Steph Scully
2=Jarrod 'Toadie' Rebecchi
   Harold Bishop
4 Charlene Robinson
5 Nell Mangel
6 Karl Kennedy
7 Declan Napier
8 Helen Daniels

Source: Yahoo Poll 2010

Steph Scully received 17% of the vote.

Kylie Minogue's character, Charlene Robinson, appeared in *Neighbours* over 20 years ago.

... Nintendo Wii Games in 2009

1 *Wii Sports Resort*
2 *Wii Fit*
3 *Wii Fit Plus*
4 *MarioKart Wii*
5 *New Super Mario Bros. Wii*
6 *Wii Play*
7 *Mario & Sonic at the Olympic Winter Games*
8 *Mario & Sonic at the Olympic Games*
9 *My Fitness Coach: Get In Shape*
10 *EA Sports Active*

11 *Carnival: Funfair Games*
12 *Just Dance*
13 *Big Beach Sports*
14 *Monopoly*
15 *Lego Star Wars: The Complete Saga*
16 *F1 2009*
17 *Super Smash Bros: Brawl*
18 *Rayman Raving Rabbids TV Party*
19 *Guitar Hero World Tour*
20 *Animal Crossing: Let's Go To The City*

Source: ELSPA/GfK Chart-Track 2009

Wii Fit is the third-bestselling console game ever, with world-wide sales of over 22 million.

The Wii balance board, looking like a set of bathroom scales, was launched in 2007.

. . . Novels

1 J.R.R. Tolkien – *The Lord of the Rings*
2 Jane Austen – *Pride and Prejudice*
3 Philip Pullman – *His Dark Materials*
4 Douglas Adams – *The Hitchhiker's Guide to the Galaxy*
5 J.K. Rowling – *Harry Potter and the Goblet of Fire*
6 Harper Lee – *To Kill a Mockingbird*
7 A.A. Milne – *Winnie-the-Pooh*

8 George Orwell – *1984*

9 C.S. Lewis – *The Lion, the Witch and the Wardrobe*

10 Charlotte Brontë – *Jane Eyre*

11 Joseph Heller – *Catch-22*

12 Emily Brontë – *Wuthering Heights*

13 Sebastian Faulks – *Birdsong*

14 Daphne du Maurier – *Rebecca*

15 J.D. Salinger – *The Catcher in the Rye*

16 Kenneth Grahame – *The Wind in the Willows*

17 Charles Dickens – *Great Expectations*

18 Louisa May Alcott – *Little Women*

19 Louis de Bernières – *Captain Corelli's Mandolin*

20 Leo Tolstoy – *War and Peace*

21 Margaret Mitchell – *Gone with the Wind*

22 J.K. Rowling – *Harry Potter and the Philosopher's Stone*

23 J.K. Rowling – *Harry Potter and the Chamber of Secrets*

24 J.K. Rowling – *Harry Potter and the Prisoner of Azkaban*

25 J.R.R. Tolkien – *The Hobbit*

26 Thomas Hardy – *Tess of the D'Urbervilles*

27 George Eliot – *Middlemarch*

28 John Irving – *A Prayer for Owen Meany*

29 John Steinbeck – *The Grapes of Wrath*

30 Lewis Carroll – *Alice's Adventures in Wonderland*

31 Jacqueline Wilson – *The Story of Tracy Beaker*

32 Gabriel García Márquez – *One Hundred Years of Solitude*

33 Ken Follett – *The Pillars of the Earth*

34 Charles Dickens – *David Copperfield*
35 Roald Dahl – *Charlie and the Chocolate Factory*
36 Robert Louis Stevenson – *Treasure Island*
37 Nevil Shute – *A Town Like Alice*
38 Jane Austen – *Persuasion*
39 Frank Herbert – *Dune*
40 Jane Austen – *Emma*
41 L.M. Montgomery – *Anne of Green Gables*
42 Richard Adams – *Watership Down*
43 F. Scott Fitzgerald – *The Great Gatsby*
44 Alexandre Dumas – *The Count of Monte Cristo*
45 Evelyn Waugh – *Brideshead Revisited*
46 George Orwell – *Animal Farm*
47 Charles Dickens – *A Christmas Carol*
48 Thomas Hardy – *Far from the Madding Crowd*
49 Michelle Magorian – *Goodnight Mister Tom*
50 Rosamunde Pilcher – *The Shell Seekers*

Source: BBC Big Read Poll 2003

J.R.R. Tolkien was Professor of Anglo-Saxon at Oxford University from 1925 to 1945. He was a friend of C.S. Lewis and took part in a literary discussion group with him called the Inklings.

The title of Philip Pullman's *His Dark Materials* comes from the poem *Paradise Lost*, written by the seventeenth-century poet John Milton.

The Nation's Favourite ...

... Online Newspapers

1 *Mail* Online
2 Guardian.co.uk
3 Telegraph.co.uk
4 *Sun* Online
5 *Times* Online
6 Mirror Group Digital
7 *Independent*

Source: ABCe 2010

Over 2 million people visit the *Daily Mail* site each day, an increase of 65% year on year.

Guardian.co.uk is visited by 1.8 million people each day, and Telegraph.co.uk by 1.6 million.

... Online Retailers

1 Amazon.co.uk
2 Argos
3 Play
4 Apple
5 Amazon.com
6 Tesco
7 Marks & Spencer
8 John Lewis
9 Next
10 EasyJet
11 Thomson Holidays
12 Expedia
13 Tesco Direct
14 ASOS
15 Thomas Cook
16 Ryanair

17 Currys	24 The Trainline
18 Debenhams	25 Comet
19 Topshop	26 Littlewoods
20 B&Q	27 River Island
21 Lastminute	28 Tesco Superstore
22 HMV	29 GAME
23 New Look	30 Asda

IMRG-Hitwise Hot Shops List February 2010

Online retailing is growing, but the rate of growth has slowed down because of the recession.

3 years ago the top 3 chart positions were held by Amazon, Argos and Tesco.

. . . Overseas Holiday Destinations

1 Spain	8 Irish Republic
2 France	9 Cyprus
3 USA	10 Netherlands
4 Italy	11 Belgium
5 Portugal	12 Germany
6 Greece	13 Caribbean
7 Turkey	

Source: ONS 2008

Over 12 million people go on holiday to Spain each year,

and 7.5 million go to France – totalling more than all the other destinations on the list combined.

The Caribbean attracts 778,000 visitors a year from the UK.

. . . Overseas Package Holiday Destinations

1 Spain	6 Portugal
2 France	7 USA
3 Greece	8 Cyprus
4 Turkey	9 Caribbean
5 Italy	10 Egypt

Source: ONS 2008

Spain attracts 4.8 million package holidaymakers from the UK each year, France 2 million, Greece 1.4 million, Turkey 1.1 million and the rest less than a million each (with Egypt attracting under half a million).

. . . Overseas Wedding Destinations

1 St Lucia	6 Las Vegas
2 Barbados	7 Jamaica
3 Mauritius	8 Seychelles
4 Antigua	9 Sri Lanka
5 Cyprus	10 Maldives

Source: American Express Travel 2006

The average UK wedding costs roughly £20,000.

The UK overseas wedding industry is worth £1.7 billion.

The Nation's Favourite . . .

. . . Painkillers

1 Nurofen
2 Lemsip
3 Anadin
4 Beechams
5 Sudafed

Source: TNS 2008

In 2002 the poet Andrew Motion admitted taking a daily dose of Lemsip to help him write poetry. He claimed that it helped him recreate 'The introverted self-pitying mood that a mild illness can give', which was in turn conducive to writing verse. A spokesman for Lemsip commented, 'It is fair to say that it doesn't cause poetry in most people.'

The first ever Beecham product was a laxative produced in St Helens, Lancashire, in 1842 made from aloe, ginger and soap.

. . . Paintings

1 J.M.W. Turner – *The Fighting Temeraire*
2 Constable – *The Hay Wain*
3 Manet – *A Bar at the Follies-Bergère*
4 Jan van Eyck – *The Arnolfini Portrait*
5 David Hockney – *Mr and Mrs Clark and Percy*

6 Vincent van Gogh – *Sunflowers*
7 Henry Raeburn – *The Reverend Robert Walker Skating on Duddingston Loch*
8 Ford Madox Brown – *The Last of England*
9 Piero della Francesca – *The Baptism of Christ*
10 William Hogarth – *A Rake's Progress*

Source: BBC 2005

The Fighting Temeraire by J.M.W. Turner received 27% of the vote. It depicts a 98-gun ship, the *Temeraire*, which had fought at the Battle of Trafalgar, on its way to be broken up. The painting hangs in the National Gallery in London.

The Hay Wain was painted in 1821. The cottage featured in the painting still exists.

. . . Party Guests

1 Jeremy Clarkson
2 Barack Obama
3 Cheryl Cole
4 Russell Brand
5 Jonathan Ross
6 Simon Cowell
7 Lewis Hamilton
8 David Beckham
9 Amy Winehouse
10 Victoria Beckham

Source: OnePoll for Heineken 2008

Jeremy Clarkson was expelled from school for drinking and smoking.

. . . PC Computer Games in 2009

1 *The Sims 3*

2 *Football Manager 2010*

3 *Football Manager 2009*

4 *Empire: Total War*

5 *Call of Duty: Modern Warfare 2*

6 *Warhammer 40,000: Dawn of War II*

7 *World of Warcraft: Wrath of the Lich King*

8 *Dragon Age: Origins*

9 *The Sims 2: Double Deluxe*

10 *The Sims 3: World Adventures*

11 *World of Warcraft: Battle Chest*

12 *World of Warcraft*

13 *Grand Theft Auto IV*

14 *Championship Manager 2010*

15 *Spore*

16 *Fallout 3*

17 *World of Warcraft: The Burning Crusade*

18 *Rollercoaster Tycoon 3*

19 *Amazing Adventures: The Lost Tomb*

20 *Call of Duty 4: Modern Warfare*

Source: ELSPA/GfK Chart-Track 2010

The first *Sims* game was released on 4 February 2000 and is the all-time bestselling PC game. It was created by Will Wright who also made the very popular *SimCity* game.

Football Manager allows the user the choice of 115 different leagues to play in.

Empire: Total War is a strategy game set in the eighteenth century.

. . . Pets

1	Fish	6	Domestic fowl
2	Dogs	7	Guinea-pigs
3	Cats	8	Hamsters
4	Rabbits	9	Horses/ponies
5	Birds	10	Tortoises/turtles

Source: PFMA 2010

Over 50 million fish are kept in the UK, compared with around 8 million dogs and almost the same number of cats.

Britons spend £520 million a year on buying cats and dogs. The average cost of a dog is £282 and of a cat £92.

Almost half of all UK cat and dog owners buy Christmas presents for their pets. The average price per present is £4.

. . . Pick-and-mix Sweets

1	Fizzy Cola bottles	6	Jelly babies
2	Cola bottles	7	Bonbons
3	Rhubarb and custards	8	Chocolate raisins
4	Wine gums	9	Chocolate eclairs
5	Black Jacks	10	Turkish delight

11	Sherbet lemons	16	Chocolate limes
12	Flying saucers	17	Chocolate coins
13	Aniseed balls	18	Percy Pigs
14	Pear drops	19	Liquorice Allsorts
15	Fruit salads	20	Apple and custards

Source: OnePoll for Marks & Spencer 2009

More women than men prefer chocolate eclairs.

Cola bottles are also called 'gummies' and are made of gelatin.

Liquorice Allsorts were created in 1899 by the sweetmakers Bassett & Co. in Sheffield.

. . . Picturesque Streets

1 The Shambles, York
2 Royal Crescent, Bath
3 Grey Street, Newcastle

Shortlist

Broad Street, Ludlow
Brunswick Square, Brighton and Hove
Chipping Campden High Street, Gloucestershire
Gold Hill, Shaftesbury, Dorset
Main Street, Tobermory, Isle of Mull
New College Lane, Oxford
Pen Cei, Aberaeron

Source: Google Street View Awards 2010

Some buildings in the Shambles date back to the fourteenth century.

The Royal Crescent in Bath was built between 1767 and 1774.

. . . Playground Games

1 Hopscotch	11 Football
2 Hide and seek	12 Blind man's bluff
3 Skipping	13 Stick in the mud
4 What's the time Mr Wolf?	14 Cops and robbers
5 British bulldog	15 The farmer's in his den
6 Conkers	16 It
7 Kiss chase	17 Elastics
8 Chinese whispers	18 Please Mr Crocodile
9 Cat's cradle	19 Jacks
10 Oranges and lemons	20 Duck, duck, goose

Source: OnePoll for TheBabyWebsite 2009

Hopscotch has been played since at least the seventeenth century. Blind man's bluff was played at the court of Henry VIII in the sixteenth century. British bulldog has been known only since the 1930s.

When you skip with two ropes it's known as Double Dutch.

. . . Poets

1 T.S. Eliot
2 John Donne
3 Benjamin Zephaniah
4 Wilfred Owen
5 Philip Larkin
6 William Blake
7 W.B. Yeats
8 John Betjeman
9 John Keats
10 Dylan Thomas

Source: BBC 2009

In a similar poll in 1995 the more traditional Rudyard Kipling poem 'If' was voted the nation's favourite.

Benjamin Zephaniah is the only living poet on the list.

. . . Pop Songs

1 Queen – 'Bohemian Rhapsody'
2 John Lennon – 'Imagine'
3 Beatles – 'Hey Jude'
4 Simon and Garfunkel – 'Bridge Over Troubled Water'
5 George Harrison – 'My Sweet Lord'
6 Procol Harum – 'A Whiter Shade Of Pale'

7 The Animals – 'The House Of The Rising Sun'

8 ABBA – 'Dancing Queen'

9 Beach Boys – 'Good Vibrations'

10 Queen and David Bowie – 'Under Pressure'

11 Kate Bush – 'Wuthering Heights'

12 Pink Floyd – 'Another Brick In The Wall'

13 Police – 'Every Breath You Take'

14 Righteous Brothers – 'You've Lost That Loving Feeling'

15 Band Aid – 'Do They Know It's Christmas'

16 Rolling Stones – '(I Can't Get No) Satisfaction'

17 Beatles – 'She Loves You'

18 Soft Cell – 'Tainted Love'

19 Beatles – 'All You Need Is Love'

20 Elvis Presley – 'Jailhouse Rock'

21 10cc – 'I'm Not In Love'

22= Steve Harley & Cockney Rebel – 'Make Me Smile (Come Up And See Me)'
   Rod Stewart – 'Maggie May'

24 Roy Orbison – 'Oh Pretty Woman'

25 David Bowie – 'Space Oddity'

26 Sinéad O'Connor – 'Nothing Compares 2 U'

27 Beatles – 'I Want To Hold Your Hand'

28 Dexy's Midnight Runners – 'Come On Eileen'

29 Marvin Gaye – 'I Heard It Through The Grapevine'

30 Monkees – 'I'm A Believer'

31 Boomtown Rats – 'I Don't Like Mondays'

32 Beatles – 'A Hard Day's Night'

33 Beatles – 'Help!'

34 Frankie Goes to Hollywood – 'Relax'
35 Kylie Minogue – 'Can't Get You Out Of My Head'
36 Queen – 'Innuendo'
37 Byrds – 'Mr Tambourine Man'
38 ABBA – 'Waterloo'
39 Elvis vs JXL – 'A Little Less Conversation'
40 Kinks – 'You Really Got Me'
41 Oasis – 'Don't Look Back In Anger'
42 Elvis Presley – 'All Shook Up'
43 Fleetwood Mac – 'Albatross'
44 Elvis Presley – 'Are You Lonesome Tonight'
45 Bryan Adams – '(Everything I Do) I Do It For You'
46 Rolling Stones – 'Paint It, Black'
47 Nilsson – 'Without You'
48 Elvis Presley – 'The Wonder Of You'
49 Louis Armstrong – 'What A Wonderful World'
50 Ian Dury & The Blockheads – 'Hit Me With Your Rhythm Stick'
51 ABBA – 'The Winner Takes It All'
52 Blondie – 'Heart Of Glass'
53 Beatles – 'Day Tripper' / 'We Can Work It Out'
54 Elvis Presley – 'Can't Help Falling In Love' / 'Rock-A-Hula Baby'
55 George Michael – 'Careless Whisper'
56=Beatles – 'Ticket To Ride'
    John Lennon – 'Woman'
58 Beatles – 'Can't Buy Me Love'
59 Elvis Presley – 'It's Now Or Never'
60 Jimi Hendrix – 'Voodoo Chile'

61 Dusty Springfield – 'You Don't Have To Say You Love Me'
62 Beatles – 'Yellow Submarine' / 'Eleanor Rigby'
63 Human League – 'Don't You Want Me'
64 Roy Orbison – 'Only The Lonely'
65 Bill Haley & His Comets – 'Rock Around The Clock'
66 Beatles – 'Paperback Writer'
67 Jam – 'Going Underground'
68 T. Rex – 'Get It On'
69 Slade – 'Merry Xmas Everybody'
70 Sonny & Cher – 'I Got You Babe'
71 Kinks – 'Sunny Afternoon'
72 Bonnie Tyler – 'Total Eclipse Of The Heart'
73=Joe Cocker – 'With A Little Help From My Friends'
   ABBA – 'Mamma Mia'
75=Gerry & The Pacemakers – 'You'll Never Walk Alone'
   David Bowie – 'Ashes To Ashes'
   Righteous Brothers – 'Unchained Melody'
78 Beatles – 'Get Back'
79 ABBA – 'Knowing Me Knowing You'
80 Madonna – 'Like A Prayer'
81 Elvis Presley – 'Return To Sender'
82 Bangles – 'Eternal Flame'
83=Freddie Mercury – 'Living On My Own'
   U2 – 'Beautiful Day'
85 Buggles – 'Video Killed The Radio Star'
86 Rolling Stones – 'Jumping Jack Flash'
87 Meat Loaf – 'I'd Do Anything For Love (But

I Won't Do That)'
88 Michael Jackson – 'Billie Jean'
89 Scott McKenzie – 'San Francisco (Be Sure To Wear Some Flowers In Your Hair)'
90 Beatles – 'From Me To You'
91 Alice Cooper – 'School's Out'
92 a-ha – 'The Sun Always Shines On TV'
93 Bee Gees – 'Night Fever'
94 Gloria Gaynor – 'I Will Survive'
95=Rolling Stones – 'Honky Tonk Women'
    Hollies – 'He Ain't Heavy, He's My Brother'
97 Beatles – 'Hello Goodbye'
98 Smokey Robinson & The Miracles – 'Tears Of A Clown'
99=Police – 'Message In A Bottle'
    Billy Joel – 'Uptown Girl'

Source: 2002 poll to commemorate the 50th Anniversary of the Official Singles Chart compiled by the Official UK Charts Company

'Bohemian Rhapsody' was released on 31 October 1975. It was number 1 for 9 weeks and has sold over a million copies.

Since 1996 'Imagine' has been played in Times Square in New York just before the New Year is rung in.

. . . Pop Videos

1 Michael Jackson – 'Thriller'
2 Peter Gabriel – 'Sledgehammer'
3 a-ha – 'Take on Me'
4 Queen – 'Bohemian Rhapsody'
5 Madonna – 'Like a Prayer'
6 Robbie Williams – 'Rock DJ'
7 Michael Jackson – 'Billie Jean'
8 The Verve – 'Bittersweet Symphony'
9 Madonna – 'Vogue'
10 Nirvana – 'Smells Like Teen Spirit'
11 Coldplay – 'The Scientist'
12 Michael and Janet Jackson – 'Scream'
13 Pink Floyd – 'Another Brick in the Wall'
14 Christina Aguilera – 'Dirrty'
15 REM – 'Everybody Hurts'
16 OutKast – 'Hey Ya'
17 Blur – 'Coffee & TV'
18 Beyoncé – 'Crazy in Love'
19 Madonna – 'Material Girl'
20 Gorillaz – 'Clint Eastwood'
21 Queen – 'I Want to Break Free'
22 Justin Timberlake – 'Cry Me a River'
23 Britney Spears – '. . . Baby One More Time'
24 Radiohead – 'No Surprises'
25 Madness – 'Baggy Trousers'
26 TLC – 'Waterfalls'
27 David Bowie – 'Ashes to Ashes'
28 Foo Fighters – 'Learn to Fly'

29 Electric Six – 'Gay Bar'

30 Weezer – 'Buddy Holly'

31 Eminem – 'Stan'

32 Chris Isaak – 'Wicked Game'

33 U2 – 'Sweetest Thing'

34 The White Stripes – 'Fell in Love with a Girl'

35 Sinéad O'Connor – 'Nothing Compares 2 U'

36 Red Hot Chili Peppers – 'Give It Away'

37 Guns N' Roses – 'November Rain'

38 Fatboy Slim – 'Weapon of Choice'

39 Pulp – 'Common People'

40 Missy Elliott – 'Get Ur Freak On'

41 The Spice Girls – 'Wannabe'

42 Björk – 'It's Oh So Quiet'

43 Dire Straits – 'Money for Nothing'

44 Kylie Minogue – 'Can't Get You Out of My Head'

45 Aerosmith – 'Crazy'

46 Adam & the Ants – 'Prince Charming'

47 The Prodigy – 'Firestarter'

48 Johnny Cash – 'Hurt'

49 Jamiroquai – 'Virtual Insanity'

50 Paul Simon – 'You Can Call Me Al'

51 Run DMC & Aerosmith – 'Walk This Way'

52 Massive Attack – 'Teardrop'

53 Wham! – 'Club Tropicana'

54 Daft Punk – 'Around the World'

55 Fatboy Slim – 'Praise You'

56 Eminem – 'Without Me'

57 Meat Loaf – 'I'd Do Anything for Love (But I Won't Do That)'

58 The Cure – 'Close to Me'

59 ABBA – 'Knowing Me, Knowing You'

60 Eurythmics – 'Sweet Dreams'

61 The Prodigy – 'Smack My Bitch Up'

62 Blur – 'Parklife'

63 George Michael – 'Outside'

64 Björk – 'Human Behaviour'

65 Aphex Twin – 'Windowlicker'

66 Bob Dylan – 'Subterranean Homesick Blues'

67 Beastie Boys – 'Sabotage'

68 Madonna – 'Ray of Light'

69 Frankie Goes to Hollywood – 'Two Tribes'

70 The Police – 'Every Breath You Take'

71 Björk – 'All Is Full of Love'

72 Robert Palmer – 'Addicted to Love'

73 Basement Jaxx – 'Where's Your Head At?'

74 Wu-Tang Clan – 'Gravel Pit'

75 Duran Duran – 'Rio'

76 The Beatles – 'Strawberry Fields Forever'

77 MC Hammer – 'U Can't Touch This'

78 Godley & Creme – 'Cry'

79 New Order – 'True Faith'

80 Radiohead – 'Just'

81 Ultravox – 'Vienna'

82 50 Cent – 'In da Club'

83 Shakespeares Sister – 'Stay'

84 The Boomtown Rats – 'I Don't Like Mondays'

85 Sid Vicious – 'My Way'

86 The Streets – 'Fit But You Know It'

87 Talking Heads – 'Once in a Lifetime'

88 Elton John – 'I Want Love'

89 Smashing Pumpkins – 'Tonight, Tonight'
90 The Pet Shop Boys – 'Go West'
91 The Specials – 'Ghost Town'
92 Herbie Hancock – 'Rockit'
93 The Rolling Stones – 'We Love You'
94 Bonnie Tyler – 'Total Eclipse of the Heart'
95 The Cardigans – 'My Favourite Game'
96 So Solid Crew – '21 Seconds'
97 Cornershop – 'Brimful of Asha'
98 Bronski Beat – 'Smalltown Boy'
99 Supergrass – 'Pumping on Your Stereo'
100 Musical Youth – 'Pass the Dutchie'

Source: Channel 4 2005

The video for Michael Jackson's 'Thriller' lasts almost 14 minutes and was directed by John Landis, who also made *An American Werewolf in London* and *The Blues Brothers*.

The turkeys in Peter Gabriel's 'Sledgehammer' were animated by Nick Park, who later created Wallace and Gromit.

. . . Post-war Prime Ministers

1 Winston Churchill
2 Clement Attlee
3 Margaret Thatcher
4 Harold Macmillan
5 Harold Wilson
6 Tony Blair

7 Edward Heath

8 John Major

9 James Callaghan

10 Alec Douglas-Home

11 Anthony Eden

12 Gordon Brown

Source: Newsnight Poll 2008

In 2002 Winston Churchill topped a BBC poll of the Greatest-ever Britons.

Clement Attlee's government created the National Health Service.

. . . Public Information Films

1 *Charley Says* series

2 *Tufty* series

3 *Joe and Petunia*

4 *Dark and Lonely Water*

5 *Green Cross Code*

6 *Reginald Molehusband*

7 *Protect and Survive*

8 *Teach Them to Swim with Rolf Harris*

9 *Clunk Click Every Trip* (Jimmy Savile)

10 *Teenagers Learn to Swim*

11 *Think Bike* (Jimmy Hill)

12 *Play Safe – Frisbee*

13=*Fireworks* (Hale and Pace)
   Bullying – Tell Someone

15 *SPLINK* (Jon Pertwee)
16 *Close to the Edges*
17 *Jobs for Young Girls*
18 *TV Licence* (Columbo)
19 *Disused Fridges*
20 *Rabies Outbreak*

Source: Central Office of Information 2006

Kenny Everett did the voices for *Charley Says*, later to be sampled by the Prodigy.

6 *Charley Says* films were made, each warning of a different danger: playing with matches, water, hot things, the kitchen, talking to strangers, and not telling Mum where you're going.

. . . Puddings

1 Apple crumble and custard
2 Strawberries and cream
3 Profiteroles
4 Chocolate fudge cake
5 Lemon meringue pie
6 Pancakes and maple syrup
7 Sticky toffee pudding
8 Ice cream
9 Treacle tart
10 Chocolate brownie

Source: Gaviscon Survey 2009

58% of people would not turn down a pudding, if offered, under any circumstances.

1% of people admitted eating their favourite pudding every day.

£1.5 billionworth of puddings were sold in 2008.

The Nation's Favourite . . .

. . . Racehorses

1	Arkle	26	Rock of Gibraltar
2	Desert Orchid	27	Double Trigger
3	Red Rum	28	Lammtarra
4	Istabraq	29	Sea-Bird
5	Brigadier Gerard	30	Mill House
6	One Man	31	West Tip
7	Persian Punch	32	Grundy
8	Dancing Brave	33	Falbrav
9	Sea Pigeon	34	Florida Pearl
10	Nijinsky	35	High Chaparral
11	Dawn Run	36	Limestone Lad
12	See More Business	37	Mtoto
13	Mill Reef	38	Montjeu
14	Best Mate	39	Pebbles
15	Wayward Lad	40	Persian War
16	Night Nurse	41	Daylami
17	Giant's Causeway	42	Edredon Bleu
18	Shergar	43	Monksfield
19	Viking Flagship	44	Burrough Hill Lad
20	Moorcroft Boy	45	Galileo
21	Crisp	46	Aldaniti
22	Nashwan	47	L'Escargot
23	Danoli	48	Pendil
24	Lochsong	49	Tingle Creek
25	Dubai Millennium	50	Triptych

Source: Racing Post 2005

The Irish racehorse Arkle is widely regarded as the greatest-ever steeplechaser. He was born in 1957 and died in 1970. He was the first horse to have a following with the general public.

Shergar won the 1981 Epsom Derby by ten lengths – the longest margin in the race's history. Two years later he was kidnapped by masked gunmen and has never been seen since.

. . . Railway Stations

1 Manchester Piccadilly
2 Glasgow Central
3 Leeds
4 Brighton
5 Edinburgh Waverley
6 London Liverpool Street
7 London Cannon Street
8 London Euston
9 London Paddington
10 London Fenchurch Street

*Source: Passenger Focus Poll 2007 (NB doesn't
include the revamped London St Pancras)*

Manchester Piccadilly recently underwent a £100 million regeneration. The station is used for 22 million journeys each year.

92% of people said they were happy with the environment of Manchester Piccadilly.

... Regional Newspapers

1 *Wolverhampton Express & Star*
2 *Liverpool Echo*
3 *Belfast Telegraph*
4 *Newcastle Evening Chronicle*
5 *Evening Times*, Glasgow
6 *Birmingham Mail*
7 *Evening Gazette*, Teesside
8 *Yorkshire Evening Post*
9 *Hull Daily Mail*
10 *Nottingham Evening Post*
11 *Edinburgh Evening News*
12 *South Wales Evening Post*

Source: ABC second half of 2009

Wolverhampton Express & Star sells just over 120,000 copies a day. It is priced at 40p.

Most regional newspapers are facing declining sales.

... Rock Gods

1 Freddie Mercury, Queen
2 Elvis Presley
3 Jon Bon Jovi, Bon Jovi
4 David Bowie
5 Jimi Hendrix, The Jimi Hendrix Experience
6 Ozzy Osbourne, Black Sabbath

7 Kurt Cobain, Nirvana

8 Slash, Guns N' Roses

9 Bono, U2

10 Mick Jagger, The Rolling Stones

11 Axl Rose, Guns N' Roses

12 Dave Grohl, The Foo Fighters

13 Jim Morrison, The Doors

14 Paul McCartney, The Beatles

15 Steven Tyler, Aerosmith

16 Robert Plant, Led Zeppelin

17 Brian May, Queen

18 James Hetfield, Metallica

19 Jimmy Page, Led Zeppelin

20 Bruce Dickinson, Iron Maiden

Source: OnePoll 2009

Queen have sold over 300 million albums.

5 of the top 20 are dead.

. . . Romantic Films

1 *Ghost*

2 *Pretty Woman*

3 *Titanic*

4 *Love Actually*

5 *Four Weddings and a Funeral*

6 *The Sound of Music*

7 *Gone with the Wind*

8 *Casablanca*
9 *Doctor Zhivago*
10 *An Officer and a Gentleman*

Source: RIAS 2008

The oldest film on the list is *Gone with the Wind*, made in 1939.

The 1990s appear to have been the golden era for romantic films, with 4 of the top 5 films having been made in that decade.

The Nation's Favourite . . .

. . . Sandwiches

1 Cheese and pickle
2 Egg mayonnaise
3 Bacon, lettuce and tomato (BLT)
4 Tuna mayonnaise
5 Cheese and tomato
6 Ham and cheese
7 Chicken salad
8 Chicken and bacon
9 Cheese and onion
10 Prawn mayonnaise
11 Cheese salad
12 Chicken and stuffing
13 Egg and bacon
14 Coronation chicken
15 King prawn and rocket
16 Ham salad
17 Ploughman's
18 Smoked salmon and cream cheese
19 Egg and cress
20 Tuna and sweetcorn

Source: OnePoll for Aldi 2009

73% of people regularly take sandwiches to work.

In 2008 the BLT topped the poll.

On average people buy one sandwich each week from a shop, and make four at home.

. . . Scenic Roads

1 A592 through the Lake District

Regionally

Midlands/North – A537 through the Peak District
North – A592 through the Lake District
Scotland – A817 Loch Lomond to Garelochhead
South East/Anglia – A35 through the New Forest
South West – B3306 between St Just and St Ives
Wales – A4086 in Snowdonia

Source: Direct Line Car Insurance YouGov 2007

The most important constituent to a great road is a coastal view, according to respondents to this survey.

89% of people say they enjoy driving, as opposed to experiencing it as stressful.

. . . Scousers

1 Wayne Rooney
2 Heidi Range
3 George Harrison
4 John Lennon

5 John Peel
6 Cilla Black
7 Ricky Tomlinson
8 Lily Savage
9 Ken Dodd
10 Jimmy Tarbuck
11 Steven Gerrard

Source: Tiscali.co.uk 2004

The two living Beatles, Ringo Starr and Paul McCartney, failed to make the list.

Heidi Range was in Atomic Kitten and is the longest-serving member of the group Sugababes.

. . . Sea Poems

1 John Masefield – 'Sea Fever'
2 Martin Newell – 'The Song of the Waterlily'
3 John Masefield – 'Cargoes'
4 Matthew Arnold – 'Dover Beach'
5 Anonymous – 'The Seafarer'
6 Charles Causley – 'Convoy'
7 Elizabeth Bishop – 'At the Fishhouses'
8 Arthur Rimbaud – 'The Drunken Boat'
9 Samuel Taylor Coleridge – 'The Rime of the Ancient Mariner'
10 Robert Louis Stevenson – 'Christmas at Sea'

Source: Magma/SeaBritain 2005

John Masefield joined the Merchant Navy at the age of 13 and sailed to Chile when he was 16, but suffered seasickness and jumped ship on his second voyage.

'Sea Fever' was published in 1900.

. . . Searched-for Names of the Noughties

1 Britney Spears
2 Osama Bin Laden
3 David Beckham
4 Princess Diana
5 Tony Blair
6 Madonna
7 Simon Cowell
8 Jade Goody
9 Madeleine McCann
10 Brad Pitt

Source: Ask Jeeves 2000–2010

In the last decade Britney Spears has been married twice and had 2 children, and suffered a breakdown in 2008. Her first album, released in 1999, . . . *Baby One More Time*, has sold over 25 million copies.

. . . Singles in 2009

1 Lady Gaga – 'Poker Face'
2 Black Eyed Peas – 'I Gotta Feeling'
3 Lady Gaga – 'Just Dance'
4 Cheryl Cole – 'Fight For This Love'
5 Joe McElderry – 'The Climb'
6 La Roux – 'In For The Kill'
7 Black Eyed Peas – 'Boom Boom Pow'
8 Rage Against The Machine – 'Killing In The Name'
9 Alexandra Burke (feat. Flo Rida) – 'Bad Boys'
10 Black Eyed Peas – 'Meet Me Halfway'

Source: The Official Chart Company 2009

Lady Gaga's 'Poker Face' stayed in the chart for 51 weeks, 2 weeks fewer than 'Just Dance'.

Joe McElderry reached number 5 although 'The Climb' was only on sale for 3 weeks.

. . . Sitcoms

1 *Only Fools and Horses*
2 *Blackadder*
3 *The Vicar of Dibley*
4 *Dad's Army*
5 *Fawlty Towers*

37 *Waiting for God*
38 *Birds of a Feather*
39 *Bread*
40 *Hi-De-Hi!*
41 *The League of Gentlemen*
42 *I'm Alan Partridge*
43 *Just Good Friends*
44 *2 Point 4 Children*
45 *Bottom*
46 *It Ain't Half Hot Mum*
47 *The Brittas Empire*
48 *Gimme Gimme Gimme*
49 *Rab C. Nesbitt*
50 *Goodnight Sweetheart*
51 *Up Pompeii!*
52 *Ever Decreasing Circles*
53 *On the Buses*
54 *Coupling*
55 *George and Mildred*
56 *A Fine Romance*
57 *Citizen Smith*
58 *Black Books*
59 *The Liver Birds*
60 *Two Pints of Lager and a Packet of Crisps*
61 *The New Statesman*
62 *Sykes*
63 *Please Sir!*
64 *Dear John*
65 *Barbara*
66 *Spaced*
67 *Bless This House*

Source: BBC 2004

A Dutch version of *Only Fools and Horses* was made called *Wat schuift't?* ('What's It Worth?'), with the Trotters renamed as the Aarsmans.

There were four series of *Blackadder*, each set during a different historical period. At various times the following periods for new series have been suggested by people associated with *Blackadder*; the 1960s, featuring a rock band called the Black Adder Five and a drummer called Bald Rick; the Second World War, Colditz as the setting; the Russian Revolution, series to be called *Red Adder*.

The character Mrs Slocombe in *Are You Being Served?* was best known for the double-entendre jokes she made about Tiddles, her cat. Typical were: 'I've got to get home. If my pussy isn't attended to by 8 o'clock, I shall be strokin' it for the rest of the evening.'

. . . Smiles

1 Kylie Minogue
2 Kelly Brook
3 Liz Hurley
4 Natalie Portman
5 Jordan

6 Serena Williams
7 Julia Roberts
8 Martine McCutcheon
9 George Clooney
10 Madonna
11 Eddie Murphy
12 Simon Cowell
13 Princess Anne
14 Jack Nicholson

Source: Tesco Personal Finance 2008

41% of people said their partner's smile brightened up their day.

People value a smile from their mother more than from their father.

. . . Soft Drinks (by type)

1 Still juice
2 Cola
3 Squash
4 Dairy and dairy substitute
5 Juice drinks
6 Plain water
7 Fruit carbonates
8 Glucose/stimulant drinks
9 Smoothies
10 Water-plus drinks

11 Lemonade

12 Non-fruit carbonates

13 Traditional mixers

14 Sports drinks

15 Cold hot drinks (tea etc.)

Source: Nielsen 2009

The above chart rates drinks by the amount of money spent on them. If we were to change it to number of litres sold Cola would be at number 1.

Sales of smoothies dropped both in volume and value by 25% in 2009.

. . . Soft Drinks (by brand)

1 Coca-Cola	6 Red Bull
2 Lucozade	7 Ribena
3 Robinson's	8 Schweppes
4 Pepsi-Cola	9 Actimel
5 Tropicana	10 Volvic

Source: Nielsen 2009

Sales of Coca-Cola are worth almost 3 times more than its nearest rival, Lucozade.

If we were to rate soft drinks in terms of volume instead of how much people spend on them, then Pepsi-Cola would be at number 2.

. . . Songs Played in the Gym

1 JLS – 'Beat Again'
2 Beyoncé – 'Sweet Dreams'
3 Dizzee Rascal – 'Holiday'
4 David Guetta – 'When Love Takes Over'
5 Pitbull – 'I Know You Want Me?'

Source: PRS Q4 2009 figures

'Beat Again' by JLS reached number 1 in the UK and sold over 100,000 copies in its first week of release.

Beyoncé's 'Sweet Dreams' stayed in the top 10 for 10 weeks.

. . . Sparkling Wines

1 Jacob's Creek
2 Codorníu
3 Marqués de Monistrol
4 Freixenet
5 Martini
6 Hardy's
7 Lindauer
8 Beringer
9 La Marca
10 Blossom Hill

Source: Nielsen 2010

£325 million was spent on sparkling wine in 2009, an increase of 12% and £1 million more than on champagne.

426,000 hectolitres of sparkling wine were drunk in the UK during 2009.

The biggest growth in popularity came from Codorníu, whose sales grew 26%.

. . . Spirits

1 Smirnoff Red Label Vodka
2 Bell's Whisky
3 Glen's Vodka
4 Famous Grouse Whisky
5 Gordon's Gin
6 Bacardi Rum
7 Jack Daniel's Whiskey
8 Baileys Irish Cream
9 High Commissioner Whisky
10 William Grant's Whisky
11 Teacher's Whisky
12 Whyte & Mackay's Whisky
13 Three Barrels Brandy
14 Courvoisier Cognac
15 Southern Comfort
16 Pimm's No. 1
17 Martell's Cognac
18 Russian Standard Vodka
19 Vodkat
20 Malibu Rum   *Source: Nielsen 2010*

Spirit sales were worth £3.18 billion in 2009, 6% up from the previous year.

3.1 million hectolitres of spirits were drunk in the UK in 2009.

Whisky is the most popular spirit, with 5 brands in the top 10, then vodka with 2, and rum and gin with 1 each.

Baileys includes some whisky, but most of its alcoholic content comes from a bacterial fermentation of whey (a by-product in the manufacture of cheese).

Glen's Vodka is made in Scotland from sugar beet rather than potatoes and is a cut-price spirit, as is the number 9 best-seller High Commissioner Whisky.

. . . Spiritual Places in the UK

1 Walsingham, Norfolk
2 Iona, Scotland
3 Avebury, Wiltshire
4 The shrine of St Alban, St Albans, Hertfordshire
5 Durham Cathedral
6 Lindisfarne, Northumberland
7 Lee Abbey, Devon
8 St David's Cathedral, St Davids, Pembrokeshire
9 St Peter's, Bradwell, Essex
10 Twyford Down, Hampshire

Source: BBC 2003

Walsingham has been a place of pilgrimage since the eleventh century, when an Anglo-Saxon noblewoman claimed she had seen a vision of the Virgin Mary.

In 563 St Columba founded a monastery on the island of Iona.

. . . Sports Commentators

1 Murray Walker (Formula 1 motor racing)
2 John Motson (football)
3 John McEnroe (tennis)
4 Peter O'Sullevan (horse racing)
5 Brian Moore (football)
6 Martin Brundle (Formula 1 motor racing)
7 Sid Waddell (darts)
8 David Coleman (football, athletics)
9 Bill McLaren (rugby)
10 Richie Benaud (cricket)
11 Dan Maskell (tennis)
12 Harry Carpenter (boxing)
13 Barry Davies (football, tennis)
14 Peter Alliss (golf)
15 Stuart Hall (football)
16 Peter Jones (football, swimming, Olympics)
17 Eddie Waring (rugby league)
18 David Vine (snooker)
19 Geoffrey Boycott (cricket)
20 Dougie Donnelly (football, snooker, darts, bowls)

Source: OnePoll for Roary the Race Car 2009

At the same time as sports-commentating, Murray Walker also worked in the advertising industry.

During a 1977 fixture between Sunderland and Tottenham Hotspur John Motson famously said, 'For those of you watching in black and white, Spurs are playing in yellow.'

. . . Sportswomen

1 Dame Kelly Holmes
2 Paula Radcliffe
3 Sally Gunnell
4 Jayne Torvill
5= Ellen MacArthur
   Dame Tanni Grey-Thompson
7 Denise Lewis
8 Rebecca Adlington
9 Tessa Sanderson
10 Zara Phillips

Source: WSFF Poll 2009 of women in sport
over the last 25 years

Kelly Holmes won gold medals in the 800 metres and 1,500 metres at the 2004 Summer Olympics in Athens.

. . . Sunday Newspapers

1 *News of the World*
2 *Mail on Sunday*
3 *Sunday Mirror*
4 *Sunday Times*
5 *Sunday Express*
6 *People*
7 *Sunday Telegraph*
8 *Sunday Mail*
9 *Daily Star Sunday*
10 *Observer*
11 *Independent on Sunday*

Source: ABC September 2009–February 2010

The *News of the World* sells almost 3 million copies each Sunday.

The *Independent on Sunday* sells 155,000 each Sunday.

The circulation of all Sunday newspapers is declining.

. . . Superstitions

1 Not walking under a ladder
2 Making a wish for good luck when blowing out birthday candles
3 Touching wood for good luck
4 Crossing fingers for good luck

5 Not putting an umbrella up in the house
6 Throwing spilt salt over left shoulder for good luck
7 Not putting shoes on the table
8 Putting money in a purse or wallet as a gift
9 Saluting a lone magpie
10 Not crossing on the stairs

Source: OnePoll for the National Lottery 2009

1 in 3 Britons won't walk under ladders or step on cracks in the pavement.

12% of people say 'White rabbits, white rabbits, white rabbits' on the 1st of the month before saying anything else.

4 out of 10 people regularly touch wood.

The Nation's Favourite . . .

. . . Takeaways

1 Chinese
2 Indian
3 Pizza
4 Fish and chips
5 Kebabs

Source: OnePoll for Aldi 2009

38% of people said they had takeaways as they couldn't be bothered to cook. 40% said they saw them as a treat.

Friday night is the most popular night of the week for a takeaway, followed by Saturday.

Britons spend £15.3 billion on takeaways each year.

. . . Theme Parks

1 Alton Towers
2 Thorpe Park
3 Cadbury World
4 Blackpool Pleasure Beach
5 Madame Tussaud's
6 Chessington World of Adventure
7 London Eye

8 London Dungeon
9 Legoland
10 Drayton Manor

Source: Yougov for Directline 2010

2.8 million people visit Alton Towers every year. It's the eleventh most visited theme park in Europe. It is owned by Merlin Entertainments, the second-largest theme park operator in the world (after Disney World). They also own Thorpe Park.

In 2009, 1.87 million people visited Thorpe Park. It was opened in 1979 and has 6 roller-coaster rides.

. . . Things about British Holidays

1 Pub lunches
2 Eating fish and chips wrapped in paper
3 Picnics in the countryside
4 Walks in the countryside
5 Eating out at a nice restaurant
6 Visiting a zoo/safari park
7 Going to a theme park
8 Cream teas
9 Going on a drive around the country
10 Going to a heritage site
11 Shopping
12 Walking around museums
13 Building sandcastles on the beach

14 Looking for creatures in rockpools
15 Camping
16 Playing crazy golf
17 Walking around stately homes
18 Outdoor swimming
19 Bike rides around the countryside
20 Going to an amusement arcade

Source: OnePoll for Tourism West Midlands 2009

95% of people said they enjoyed going on holiday in the UK.

92% said they would like to try a new activity, watersports being the top choice.

. . . Things to Moan About

1 Bad weather
2 Tiredness
3 Rubbish TV
4 Slow Internet connections
5 How messy home is
6 Traffic
7 Workload
8 Hangovers
9 Rude shop assistants
10 Feeling ill
11 Queue jumpers
12 The recession/credit crunch
13 Being hungry

14 Automated phone systems
15 Headaches
16 Neighbours
17 Cold-callers
18 Slow walkers
19 An annoying boss
20 Price of petrol

Source: OnePoll for Uniroyal Tyres 2009

Typically, a British person moans 4 times a day.

8% of people said they moaned because they enjoyed doing it.

37% said they moan simply to start a conversation.

. . . Time for Sex

1 Saturday night, 10.16 p.m.
2 Friday night, 9 p.m.
3 Sunday morning, 9.30 a.m.

Source: OnePoll 2009

The average duration of sex on Saturday night is 19 minutes.

70% of people claim to be happy with their sex lives.

. . . TV Cars

1 KITT from *Knight Rider*
2 Inspector Morse's Jaguar Mk2
3 The Ferrari Testarossa from *Miami Vice*
4 *Magnum, PI's* Ferrari 308
5 The Batmobile from *Batman*
6 Gene Hunt's Audi Quattro from *Ashes to Ashes*
7 FAB1, Lady Penelope's Rolls-Royce from *Thunderbirds*
8 The General Lee Dodge Charger from *The Dukes of Hazzard*
9 The Saint's Volvo P1800
10 The A-Team's GMC Vandura van

Source: KwikFit 2010

KITT starred in the David Hasselhoff series *Knight Rider* and is short for Knight Industries Two Thousand. It was a 1982 Pontiac Firebird. The car's famous voice was provided by the actor William Daniels.

KITT came top with 18% of the vote, Inspector Morse's Jaguar was close behind with 16%, but the rest got 8% or less.

. . . TV Catchphrases

1 'D'Oh!' – *The Simpsons*
2 'Yabba-Dabba-Doo!' – *The Flintstones*

3 'Exterminate!' – *Doctor Who*

4 'Beam me up Scotty!' – *Star Trek*

5 'To me, to you' – *Chucklevision*

6 'By the power of Grayskull!' – *He-Man and the Masters of the Universe*

7 'I love it when a plan comes together' – *The A-Team*

8 'Fan–dabi–dozi!' – *The Krankies*

9 'I pity the fool!' – *The A-Team*

10 'What's up, Doc?' – *Bugs Bunny*

11 'I tawt I taw a puddy tat' – Tweety Pie on *Looney Tunes*

12 'Oh my God, they killed Kenny!' – *South Park*

13 'Whatchu talkin' 'bout Willis?' – *Diff'rent Strokes*

14 'If it wasn't for you meddling kids' – *Scooby Doo, Where Are You!*

15 'Can we fix it? Yes we can!' – *Bob the Builder*

16 'Is it a bird, is it a plane? No it's Superman!' – *Superman*

17 'Ooh I could crush a grape!' – *Crackerjack*

18 'Eat my shorts' – *The Simpsons*

19 'Here's another fine mess you've gotten me into' – Laurel and Hardy

20 'Cowabunga Dude!' – *Teenage Mutant Ninja Turtles*

Source: OnePoll for TheBabyWebsite 2009

In 1998 'Doh!' was added to *The New Oxford Dictionary of English* and defined as 'used to comment on an action perceived as foolish or stupid'.

The catchphrase 'Yabba-Dabba-Doo!' mimicked a Brylcreem advertising jingle, 'A Little Dab'll Do Ya!'

. . . TV Characters

1 Homer Simpson
2 Basil Fawlty
3 Blackadder
4 Del Boy
5 Father Dougal
6 Doctor Who
7 Alan Partridge
8 Ali G
9 Victor Meldrew
10 Dr Niles Crane (*Frasier*)
11 Jim Royle
12 B.A. Baracus
13 The Fonz
14 Rick (*The Young Ones*)
15 Kevin the Teenager
16 Tubbs (*Miami Vice*)
17 Alan B'Stard
18 Columbo
19 Ted and Ralph
20 Patsy Stone
21 Captain Mainwaring
22 Frank Spencer
23 Mr Spock
24 Rigsby
25 Ally McBeal
26 Norman Stanley Fletcher (*Porridge*)
27 The Prisoner
28 Dennis Pennis
29 Miss Piggy

30 Inspector Morse

31 Sir Humphrey Appleby

32 Bilko

33 Emma Peel

34 Compo

35 Hawkeye

36 Fitz (*Cracker*)

37 Arthur Daley

38 J. R. Ewing

39 Albert Steptoe

40 Rab C. Nesbitt

41 Stuart Jones (*Queer as Folk*)

42 Frost

43 Arnold (*Happy Days*)

44 Margot Leadbetter (*The Good Life*)

45 Huggy Bear

46 Dot Cotton

47 Beth Jordache

48 Desmond

49 Alf Garnett

50 Anna Forbes (*This Life*)

51 Hancock

52 Hyacinth Bucket

53 Mrs Overall

54 Mrs Merton

55 Oz

56 Kojak

57 Yosser Hughes

58 Terry Collier

59 Dame Edna Everage

60 Wolfie Smith

61 Charlene
62 Claudius
63 Mr Humphries
64 Max Headroom
65 F. Urquhart
66 Hilda Ogden
67 Dorien
68 Pete
69 Jack Regan
70 Jimmy Corkhill
71 Napoleon Solo
72 Loadsamoney
73 Lurcio
74 Jack Duckworth
75 Den & Angie
76 Beverley
77 Simon Templar
78 Jane Tennison
79 Bet Lynch
80 Sid Abbott
81 Kim Tate
82 Quentin Crisp
83 Lucy
84 Darius Jedbergh
85 Mildred Roper
86 Jason King
87 Jill Munroe
88 Delbert Wilkins
89 Philip Marlowe
90 Michael Murray
91 Hudson

92 Benny
93 Keith Pratt
94 Charlie Barlow
95 Hari Kumar
96 Reggie Perrin
97 Peter Manson
98 Buffy
99 Brian Potter
100 Budgie

Source: Channel 4 2001

Only 12 half-hour episodes of *Fawlty Towers* were ever made.

Dr Niles Crane is the highest-placed American in this list, an achievement made all the greater by the fact that he is not the lead character in *Frasier*.

. . . TV Dogs

1 Lassie
2 Scooby Doo
3 Brian (*Family Guy*)
4 Hobo (*Littlest Hobo*)
5 Shep (*Blue Peter*)
6 Well'Ard (*EastEnders*)
7 K9 (*Doctor Who*)
8 Santa's Little Helper (*The Simpsons*)
9 Bouncer (*Neighbours*)
10 Snoopy

Source: OnePoll for The Dog Whisperer 2008

Lassie first appeared in a 1938 short story 'Lassie Come Home' by Eric Knight. It was made into a movie starring Elizabeth Taylor and Roddy McDowall in 1943.

50% of people enjoy watching TV with their dog.

1 in 4 people leaves the TV on when they go out so that their dog can watch.

. . . TV Dramas in 2009

1 *Doc Martin*
2 *Doctor Who*
3 *Jonathan Creek*
4 *Whitechapel*
5 *New Tricks*
6 *Wild at Heart*
7 *Collision*
8 *Above Suspicion*
9 *Ashes to Ashes*
10 *Unforgiven*

Source: BARB 1 January–29 November 2009

6 of the top 10 were shown on ITV, the other 4 were first broadcast on BBC1.

The most popular new drama was *Whitechapel*, followed by (in decreasing popularity) *Collision*, *Above Suspicion*, *Unforgiven*, *Murderland*, *Law and Order: UK*, *Demons*, *Hope Springs*, *Hunter* and *Life of Riley*.

. . . TV Mums

1 Marge Simpson (*The Simpsons*)
2 Pamela Shipman (*Gavin and Stacey*)
3 Susan Harper (*My Family*)
4 Linda Bellingham (Oxo advert)
5 Ma Larkin (*The Darling Buds of May*)
6 Barbara Royle (*The Royle Family*)
7 Susan Kennedy (*Neighbours*)
8 Peggy Mitchell (*EastEnders*)
9 Hyacinth Bucket (*Keeping Up Appearances*)
10 Lisa Dingle (*Emmerdale*)

Source: Vouchercodes.co.uk 2010

Marge Simpson is named after *The Simpsons* creator Matt Groening's mother Margaret.

Pamela Shipman is played by Alison Steadman, best known for her role as Beverly in Mike Leigh's play *Abigail's Party*.

. . . TV Shows in 2009

1 *Britain's Got Talent Final Result*
2 *The X Factor Results*
3 *EastEnders*
4 *Coronation Street*
5 *Dancing on Ice*
6 *I'm A Celebrity, Get Me Out of Here!*
7 *Doc Martin*

8 *Strictly Come Dancing*
9 *Children in Need*
10 *Doctor Who*

Source: *BARB figures for 2009 to 29 November*

The *Britain's Got Talent* final was watched by 18.2 million people, while 15 million enjoyed the *X Factor* final.

Doc Martin was the most popular drama series, with an audience of 10.2 million.

. . . TV Theme Tunes

1 *Only Fools and Horses*
2 *Minder*
3 *Doctor Who*
4 *Match of the Day*
5 *EastEnders*
6 *The A-team*
7 *Friends*
8 *The Pink Panther*
9 *Ski Sunday*
10 *Coronation Street*

Source: *OnePoll 2009*

The writer and performer of the theme tune of *Only Fools and Horses*, John Sullivan, also created the drama. The tune figured from the second series onwards.

The opening music to *Minder*, 'I Could Be So Good For You', was written by Dennis Waterman's wife Patricia. It got to number 3 in the charts in November 1980.

The *Doctor Who* theme was composed by Ron Grainer and recorded by Delia Derbyshire at the BBC Radiophonic Workshop in 1963.

The Nation's Favourite . . .

. . . UK Beach Resorts

1 Southwold, Suffolk
2 Newquay, Cornwall
3 Scarborough, Yorkshire
4 Bournemouth, Dorset
5 Brighton, Sussex
6 Blackpool, Lancashire
7 Skegness, Lincolnshire
8 Torquay, Devon
9 Rhyl, Denbighshire
10 Dunoon, Argyll

Source: Teletext Holidays 2007

Just outside the top 10 came Southend, Padstow, Barmouth, Salcombe and Weston-super-Mare.

People liked Southwold because of its beach huts, fish and chip shops and its lighthouse. Newquay was favoured for its watersports and scenery, while Bournemouth was picked on account of its 7-mile beach.

. . . UK Holiday Destinations

1 Cornwall
2 Devon and Somerset
3 The Lake District

4 Blackpool and the North West
5 London
6 The South Coast
7 Scotland
8 Yorkshire and the North East
10 Wales

Source: Teletext Holidays 2010

60% of survey respondents aged under 30 thought UK beach resorts were unfashionable.

Favourite UK city-break destinations for the under-30s are Bournemouth, Edinburgh and Brighton.

Favourite UK coastal resorts for the over-60s are Blackpool, Torquay and St Ives.

. . . Used Cars

1 Vauxhall Corsa
2 Ford Fiesta
3 Vauxhall Astra
4 Ford Focus
5 Volkswagen Golf
6 BMW 3 series
7 Ford Mondeo
8 Renault Clio
9 Vauxhall Vectra
10 Peugeot 206   *Source: Experian 2009*

In 2008 the Vauxhall Astra was the bestselling car, the Ford Fiesta was number 2 and the Vauxhall Corsa number 3.

The top-selling 4x4 was the Land Rover Freelander; the top-selling sports car, the Audi TT; and the top-selling MPV, the Vauxhall Zafira.

The Nation's Favourite . . .

. . . Valentine's Dates

Female

1 Cheryl Cole
2 Jennifer Aniston
3 Keira Knightley
4 Angelina Jolie
5 Megan Fox

Male

1 George Clooney
2 Robbie Williams
3 Brad Pitt
4 Johnny Depp

Source: LateRooms.com 2010

The first record of St Valentine's Day, 14 February, being associated with romantic love comes in the fourteenth-century writings of Geoffrey Chaucer.

George Clooney got 21% of the vote; Cheryl Cole got 9%.

. . . Vegetables

1 Onion
2 Sweetcorn
3 Carrot
4 Pepper
5 Brussels sprout

6 Garlic
7 Pea
8 Spinach
9 Bean
10 Courgette

Source: Dolmio Foods Survey 2005

55% of people voted for the onion. Sweetcorn, at number 2, got only 18%.

Men prefer to boil vegetables while women prefer to steam them.

Only 14% of 16- to 24-year-olds said they would be happy trying a vegetable they had never tasted before.

The Nation's Favourite . . .

. . . Wearers of Glasses

1 Elton John
2 John Lennon
3 Dame Edna Everage
4 Gok Wan
5 Eric Morecambe
6 Alan Carr
7 Timmy Mallett
8 The Queen
9 Johnny Depp
10 Jarvis Cocker
11 David Tennant (as Doctor Who)
12 Anastacia
13 Harry Hill
14 Anne Robinson
15 Penfold (*Danger Mouse*)
16 Daniel Radcliffe
17 Nicky Hambleton-Jones
18 Rolf Harris
19 Samuel L. Jackson
20 Cheryl Cole

Source: OnePoll for Specsavers 2009

John Lennon was known for his round gold-rimmed glasses similar to a type then provided by the NHS. Sunglasses in the same style are known as 'teashades'.

Elton John is known for wearing flamboyant glasses. So far he has owned over 20,000 pairs.

Dame Edna's cat's-eye diamanté glasses are an essential part of the costume worn by Australian comedian Barry Humphries when playing that character.

. . . Websites to Watch Videos On

1	YouTube	6	Channel 4
2	BBC	7	Dailymotion
3	Megavideo	8	ITV
4	Facebook	9	Blinkx
5	Microsoft	10	Sky

Source: comScore 2009

Online viewing in the UK grew by 37% in 2009.

YouTube grew by 17% in the UK in 2009.

43 million videos were viewed on Facebook, an increase of 205% on 2008.

. . . Welsh People

1 Ray Gravell
2 Katherine Jenkins
3 Joe Calzaghe

Source: Welsh Assembly Poll 2008

Rugby player Ray Gravell got 21% of the vote, singer Katherine Jenkins 15% and boxer Calzaghe 13%.

Other shortlisted names were Tom Jones, Bryn Terfel, Gethin Jones, Ryan Giggs, James Hook, St David and Hywel Dda.

. . . Whiskies

1 Glenfiddich
2 Glenmorangie Original
3 Glenlivet
4 Glenmorangie 10 year old
5 Laphroaig
6 Highland Park
7 Aberlour
8 Glen Moray
9 Isle of Jura
10 Talisker

Source: The Grocer 2008

Sales of Glenfiddich increased by 24% in 2008, putting it above its rival Glenmorangie which had been the top-selling brand for the previous 13 years. Glenfiddich is owned by William Grant & Sons Ltd, the third-largest producer of Scotch whisky.

Glenmorangie is the bestselling blended whisky. It is owned by the luxury goods company Moët Hennessy Louis Vuitton.

. . . Wines

1. Blossom Hill
2. Hardy's
3. Gallo
4. Jacob's Creek
5. Lindemans
6. Echo Falls
7. First Cape
8. Kumala
9. Stowells
10. Wolf Blass
11. Isla Negra
12. Concha y Toro
13. J.P. Chenet
14. Banrock Station
15. Oyster Bay
16. Namaqua
17. Rosemount
18. Ogio
19. Canti
20. Arniston Bay

Source: Nielsen 2010

Sales of First Cape grew by 60% in 2009.

The average price of wine is £4.32. The most expensive of the top 10 brands is Jacob's Creek, whose average price is £5.15p.

8.9 million hectolitres of wine were drunk in the UK in 2009, 3% up on the previous year.

. . . Wits

1. Oscar Wilde
2. Spike Milligan
3. Stephen Fry
4. Jeremy Clarkson

5 Sir Winston Churchill
6 Paul Merton
7 Noël Coward
8 William Shakespeare
9 Brian Clough
10 Liam Gallagher

Source: UKTV 2007

Spike Milligan had 'I told you I was ill' engraved on his tombstone.

Wilde on writing books: 'In old days books were written by men of letters and read by the public. Nowadays books are written by the public and read by nobody.'

Sir Winston Churchill, when asked what qualities a politician required, answered: 'The ability to foretell what is going to happen tomorrow, next week, next month, and next year – and the ability afterwards to explain why it didn't happen.'

. . . Women's Magazines

1 *Glamour*
2 *Cosmopolitan*
3 *Good Housekeeping*
4 *Woman and Home*
5 *Look*
6 *Prima*
7 *Yours*

8 *Marie Claire*
9 *Candis*
10 *Company*
11 *Grazia*
12 *Red*
13 *Vogue*
14 *Elle*
15 *More!*
16 *InStyle*
17 *Easy Living*
18 *She*
19 *BM*
20 *Psychologies*
21 *Essentials*
22 *Harper's Bazaar*
23 *Vanity Fair*
24 *Tatler*
25 *Ladies First*

Source: ABC July–December 2009

Glamour sold 515,000 copies. Both *Cosmopolitan* and *Good Housekeeping* sold 430,000.

The women's magazine sector is still growing – circulation was 9.5% higher in this period than in the first half of 2009.

The fastest-growing title is *Essentials*, which has gained 13.9% year on year, although its circulation is still only 112,135 each month.

... World Cup Songs

1 The Lightning Seeds – 'Three Lions'
2 New Order – 'World In Motion'
3 Fat Les – 'Vindaloo'
4 England World Cup Squad – 'Back Home'
5 Embrace – 'World At Your Feet'
6 Ant & Dec – 'We're On The Ball'
7 Luciano Pavarotti – 'Nessun dorma'
8 Andy Cameron – 'Ally's Tartan Army'
9 England World Cup Squad – 'This Time We'll Get It Right'
10 Dario G – 'Carnaval de Paris'

Source: PRS 2010

75% of people believe that a rousing song boosts player morale.

65% of people believe it is important to have a national song to raise the crowd's emotions.

'Three Lions' has been popular internationally, reaching number 16 on the German pop chart in 1996.

The Nation's Favourite . . .

. . . Xbox 360 Games

1 *Call of Duty: Modern Warfare 2*
2 *FIFA 10*
3 *Forza Motorsport 3*
4 *Assassin's Creed II*
5 *Halo 3: ODST*
6 *Call of Duty: World at War*
7 *Resident Evil 5*
8 *Lego Batman: The Videogame*
9 *Grand Theft Auto: Episodes from Liberty City*
10 *Left 4 Dead 2*
11 *Pure*
12 *Call of Duty 4: Modern Warfare*
13 *Need for Speed: Shift*
14 *Gears of War 2*
15 *Halo Wars*
16 *FIFA 09*
17 *Batman: Arkham Asylum*
18 *UFC 2009: Undisputed*
19 *Grand Theft Auto IV*
20 *Halo 3*

Source: ELSPA/GfK Chart-Track 2009

Over 40 million Xbox 360s have been sold worldwide since their launch in 2005.

The Xbox 360 is also notorious for the 'red ring of death', when 3 of the lights around the power button flash, indicating a general hardware failure.

The Nation's Favourite . . .

. . . YouTube Videos

1 'Évian Roller Babies' – Évian advert
2 'Extreme Sheep LED Art' – Samsung advert
3 'YouTube Street Fighter' – recreation of video game using model figures
4 'Damien Walters Showreel 2009' – acrobatic free runner
5 'Simon's Cat "Fly Guy"' – comedy animation

Source: YouTube 2009

In 2009 the most popular video worldwide was Susan Boyle's, with 120 million views; the most popular music video was Pitbull's 'I Know You Want Me'.

Damien Walters is a former tumbling champion turned free runner who now works as a stuntman. The release of his annual showreel has become a much anticipated YouTube event.

Acknowledgements

I would like to thank my agent Simon Benham of Mayer Benham, my brother Ewan for letting me work in his flat, my wife Gemma, Sue Phillpott, my publisher Richard Milner and all at Quercus.

I can be contacted on thenationsfavourite@yahoo.co.uk